THE SECRET LIFE OF POP-UPS

A Practical Guide To Elevate Your Community Engagement

CINDY PLOWMAN

First published by Ultimate World Publishing 2025
Copyright © 2025 Cindy Plowman

ISBN

Paperback: 978-1-923255-99-9
Ebook: 978-1-923425-00-2

Cover design: Ultimate World Publishing
Layout and typesetting: Ultimate World Publishing
Editor: Carmela Julian Valencia

Ultimate World Publishing
Diamond Creek,
Victoria Australia 3089
www.writeabook.com.au

ULTIMATE WORLD
PUBLISHING

Testimonials

"Watching Cindy pour her heart into this book has been truly inspiring. She's always had this incredible ability to connect with people, whether it's through her work or over a cup of coffee. What she's created here is a reflection of her passion for bringing people together and making their voices heard. This book is Cindy at her best—practical, insightful, and full of stories that remind us of the power of genuine connection."

"Working alongside Cindy has been an education in itself. Her ability to take complex challenges and turn them into meaningful engagement opportunities is remarkable. This book captures the essence of her approach—creative, innovative, and grounded in real-world experience. It's not just a guide for professionals; it's a masterclass in how to make a difference through community engagement."

"I've seen firsthand the dedication Cindy puts into everything she does. This book is a culmination of years of hard work, late nights, and her unwavering belief in the power of community. She's taken the lessons she's learned in the field and turned them into something that's not only practical but also deeply inspiring. I couldn't be prouder of what she's achieved."

"Cindy has always been the person who lights up a room and makes everyone feel like their voice matters. This book is so 'her'—a perfect mix of wit, wisdom, and heart. I've watched her grow into this incredible professional who doesn't just talk about making a difference but actually does it. This book is a gift to anyone looking to create meaningful change."

"Cindy's leadership has transformed how we approach community engagement. She's not just a boss; she's a mentor who empowers everyone around her to think bigger and do better. This book feels like an extension of that mentorship—a resource that shares her unique insights and gives others the tools to elevate their work. It's a must-read for anyone in the field."

Dedication

To my family, who instilled in me the values of curiosity and hard work; to my mum, for always reminding me I could do anything; and to Drew, for joining me on this wild caravan journey.

For everyone working tirelessly in community engagement – you are the heartbeat of meaningful change.

'Unless someone like you cares an awful lot, nothing is going to get better. It's not.' – Dr. Seuss

Contents

Introduction: My why

Pop ups are not that user-friendly. Often it means working weekends, being out in the elements, lugging stools, tables and marquees around in your car, and holding on until you find a toilet (or a clean one, anyway). Personally, I've been told to fuck off, reminded that my wage is being paid for by the ratepayer, or avoided – head down, fake phone call, no eye contact, hustled past style.

While all these are formative experiences that have shaped who I am today (and will be ever grateful for), I want to help you and others avoid the pain of having these experiences and get it right from the start.

Pop ups provide an essential opportunity for people to share ideas with those in power, have their questions answered and their beliefs checked all the while shaping the cities we live in, the policies we abide by and adding to the rich fabric of life we fortunately know in Australia.

I imagine you are in one of two camps – you either dig pop ups and want to get better, or find them super difficult and want them to suck less. I've got you both covered!

I need to admit something about myself: The Conversation Caravan you see today was born from a loathing of pop ups and, in fact, community engagement as a whole. I initially purchased and started renovating the caravan with the idea of creating a cocktail van. I was ready to trade my Post-it notes for a cocktail swizzle stick! I had given up on community engagement and, in particular, face-to-face engagement. Working within a local council, I found the project teams I was supporting moving further away from using in-person methods; there were more online surveys or badly written letters posted out to residents.

Every time we went out to the community we got harassed, and it was too difficult to get people to work on weekends or after hours or to lug equipment around with them.

We were also making our community angrier it seemed. Our satisfaction scores for community engagement and trust scores were dropping, and it all felt like a hot mess! Ten years in at that point, I thought I was done. It's been good, but maybe I need to return to my event management origins; be with (mostly happy) drunk people again.

Still wanting to work with people (with a side of cocktails), I studied change management and neurolinguistic programming and learnt more about the science of how people change and human behaviour patterns. Still with my exit planned, I started using what I was learning in these courses – recognising learning patterns (*Boom!* Less frustration.), speaking to participant core needs (less anger), understanding myself better and tendencies (personally less frustrated). This is explored more in Chapter 8: 'Engage Human Nature'.

Moving through my own stages of grief – from feeling like I know something, then realising I know nothing, to feeling guilty because I am my organisation's expert – I started embedding more of these changes into our organisation's practice and re-believing that maybe I could make a difference. It is possible to bring people and decision-makers together, to think through the issues we're facing and work through these to the point of getting a win-win situation. All while standing on the street.

I love being in business. I still wanted to quit my day job but my husband is not a camper, so I had to find an alternative use for my caravan. I was fortunate to have some wonderful friends and peers who initially hired me and my now-consultation caravan, which had a very impressive bar fridge and stainless steel sink (perhaps more than was needed to consult on a health plan).

On my first pop up event with April (our van) we had people flock to us on a quiet country street in Timboon, Victoria. We had farmers come and sit in the van and talk to us about their health. They'd not seen timber windows like that in a caravan (Thanks, Uncle Fred) or the curved design of the room (Thanks, husband). It became a talking point, with a side of sharing feedback.

Enthusiasm renewed! Thinking cap on: People are drawn to vibrant colours and attractive things that look interesting. We began creating props and backdrops and purchased equipment and bright colour furnishings.

Today I see our props and April being used as the backdrop to draw people towards us, to give our project teams and technical leads something they can stand in front of and be proud of, as opposed to standing in a public place with a trestle table, looking like a telemarketer or fundraiser (no offence, we each have our place). It is far more heartwarming speaking to people who gravitate to you than replying 'Not interested'.

I want to share what I've learnt and what we've put in place to strengthen our practice.

I have written this book for the internal expert, the person who sits within their organisation tasked with the massive job of supporting teams to deliver good engagement, who reports on the mess-ups to the CEO and the mix-ups to the project director and who, still with open arms, welcomes back the traffic engineer who created the communications nightmare in the first place. All the while believing in their heart that there has to be a better way, that community and stakeholder wisdom really can positively impact the work delivered and decisions made.

I see you and want to make your work more enjoyable.

This book is written in a way you can start making the changes within each chapter. I would prefer you to do the action rather than absorb the knowledge with inaction.

My favourite chapters that are a little heavier, in the long run, will make a big difference:
- Chapter 1: 'Keep yourself and others safe'
- Chapter 7: 'Work to your team's strength'
- Chapter 8: 'Engage human nature'
- Chapter 9: 'Rooms within rooms'

What we still spend a lot of focus on when I work with our clients and need to continue to work on as an industry:

- Chapter 2: 'Connecting your pop up to your program'
- Chapter 4: 'Make making sense easy'

Lighter chapters that will make your life easier:
- Chapter 5: 'Selecting the right location'
- Chapter 11: 'We're not selling anything'

Within each chapter, there are a few action steps with links to download some tools and resources to help you on your path.

Chapter 1

Keep yourself and others safe

In Australia, over a third of workers have experienced some form of work-related violence or aggression.[1] I am leading with this chapter, as our industry (civic professionals) is in the top three industries with the highest frequency rate of work-related harassment and/or bullying, behind 'public order and safety services' and 'residential care services'.[2] And the rate of claims was more than twice as high for women as men.

In my experience, the number one fear project leads have when working in stakeholder and community engagement is being approached with anger, distrust or abuse. These experiences, perceived or real, can mean that project teams select less impactful methods for engaging – hiding their project, their work and their expertise behind a corporate website with a link

---

[1] The frequency rate is the number of accepted claims per 100 million hours worked.

[2] Psychosocial health and safety and bullying in Australian workplaces, Safe Work Australia, 2021.

to a one-dimensional survey. No one benefits from this. Those impacted and even interested in the potential of the project are not scrolling through the website daily, checking for updates and (without extensive promotion) are not going to stumble on the link to provide feedback or their lived experience or expressed needs. Nor do the project teams and subject matter experts have the opportunity to share their industry knowledge, the research and nuanced detail that went into the work. Instead, we reinforce a biased and commonly held view among project teams: 'The general community is not interested in [insert whichever subject matter your project is about]', which leaves us, the **professional people whisperers**, feeling frustrated and annoyed about how we encourage better connection and communication between community and decision-makers.

Pop ups (going to where the community are in a fun and engaging way) have the potential to bring people together, generate interest and create a genuine dialogue between the community and our technical experts to enrich understanding on both sides and ultimately result in better and well-informed and considered decisions. This will only work if pop ups are designed in a psychologically safe manner.

In this chapter (really, this book) you will learn how to plan and deliver pop up events in a psychologically safe manner to create an environment that protects the wellbeing of the staff and encourages the community to bring their best selves to the conversations while having their needs and answers met.

Before we dive into the strategies to guide and defuse conversations in the community, we need to know why it is so important to get this right. Specifically, we need to:

- give staff the tools to protect themselves from work-related harassment and/or bullying
- remove the fear of conflict and need to manage off-topic conversations that stop project teams from delivering in-person engagement
- create a safe space for the community to share their views and experiences, and leave with a better connection to the project and your organisation
- instil credibility in the work we do as community engagement practitioners or as an organisation by handling it well.

If we don't get this right, we may:
- set up staff for ongoing harassment (In the past, we have had community members follow our staff and turn up to every event)
- see project teams and subject matter experts default to using more impersonal engagement tools that require less discussion
- make living in a small (or not so small) community untenable for participants in our process – particularly where there is a clear divide on the subject of discussion or varying degrees of impact – therefore creating an experience that singles out individuals and their point of view, making them unpopular in their own community.

As practitioners, we can focus too heavily on managing conflict, to the point of designing it out or avoiding situations or conversations that might elicit it. Yet, conflict can be the bump in the road on the way to a change in opinion, learning something new, having your world view changed or your technical expertise questioned or critiqued. Rather than designing out conflict, the goal should be the psychological safety of both the staff member or project teams and our community or professional stakeholders.

Psychological safety means creating an environment where it is okay to express ideas and concerns, speak up with questions and admit mistakes – all without fear of negative consequences. Psychological safety leads people to feel more engaged and motivated because they feel their contributions matter and they're able to speak up without fear of retribution. Second, it can lead to better decision-making, as people feel more comfortable voicing their opinions and concerns, which often leads to a more diverse range of perspectives being heard and considered.

In this chapter, I want to give you some tools to:
- establish clear boundaries and protocols to keep yourself and others safe
- plan for the role you are providing (Is it community engagement or customer service) and recognise the role
- manage off-topic conversations and high emotions to get the conversation back to that sweet spot
- make psychological safety the norm within your organisation (agreed practice, policy, debriefing, incident reporting and welfare support).

'I'm freaking out!' Early in my career, a community member said this to me moments before they physically assaulted someone after overhearing their differing opinion. Knowing I could have stopped this from happening still plays on my mind on repeat. I, of course, tried to out-explain the freak-out, shove more information at the fire and hope it would disappear. It didn't. It stoked it and, of course, the flames erupted into surrounding areas. I don't want you to have this same regret in your professional subconscious.

Why we react the way we do

I lost my bundle when my husband used my favourite fry pan. A friend living with us was witness to this and afterwards said, 'I can see why your relationship works, but it's not one I would like.' Some 12 years later he still brings it up.

I can't remember why I reacted, but I know I react when I have a picture of how something will work in my mind and it doesn't, I am tired or hungry, I feel like I am losing control, I don't understand something and don't have the time to learn or understand it, I feel embarrassed or ashamed, and my family or friends are under threat or being disrespected. I'm sure you're thinking surely these things happen on a frequent basis, yet I am not in the news, running around the suburb like the Hulk smashing into things. It's the stacking of these events that create the fuel for the fire that, if triggered through a stimulus, situation or event, can prompt the reaction.

Why do people react the way they do? Simple answer. We are **all** under pressure from the multiple daily hats we wear – be that in our family, extended family, at our work, where we volunteer, with our neighbours and, if we have cultural ties, cultural norms and values.

We all overcommit. We all have some kind of past trauma. We all have insecurities. We all have hopes and dreams. Some of us have injuries or illnesses that create another layer of complexity.

I'd prefer that you approach this topic with self-awareness and empathy; however, understand the need for more schooled reasoning. Organisation Development Theory is perhaps the most researched and discussed approach to conflict. It presents two categories of conflict:

- **Affective Conflict** stems from emotional or personal disagreements due to individual or group differences and preferences, usually around the why or how of a project. It is often characterised by raised negative emotions, high tensions and hostility among the parties involved.
- **Task Conflict** (also called Cognitive or Functional Conflict) stems from disagreement on the what, when and why of a task or project. This type of conflict can have its benefits, especially in its early stages where it can foster constructive discussions or a change of project direction.

Using this in our practice, an example of affective conflict can be seen in hyperlocalised debates about car parking and the possible reallocation of car parking for public open space, bike paths or vegetation. This subject tends to bring in a clash of values – if the individual sees other road users as equal or higher priority, if the individual sees themselves aligned to living a sustainable lifestyle, if the individual is reliant on car parking for easy access and lifestyle needs, if the individual feels they have lacked a voice in the past about this subject, or if this change in land use is even required.

Meanwhile, the most common examples of task conflict are:
- Timing of engagement – too short, during a holiday period.
- Engagement process – inadequate communications, opportunities to engage and the methods selected for engaging.
- Misinformation – from the project team or within the community, different information or references cited.

Start with yourself, it's easier

We need to manage ourselves and our own reactions. We need to know our triggers, have strategies in place for these and know our boundaries and the confidence and organisational support to enact these.

When facilitating a workshop, the client asked me if I could remind participants about the need to be respectful to staff. The room was working in small groups at the time, and so I immediately jumped into action, asking a series of follow-up questions to understand the behaviour, conversations or complaints this person had heard or seen, to which they replied, 'The participant was rolling their eyes.'

Now, as someone with very expressive eyebrows, at times they wander too close to my forehead or the bridge of my nose, eye rolling is not an issue for me. For my client, this was a trigger that was causing them an Affective Conflict Response. While it's great to notice the participant was perhaps feeling frustration, reframing this – it could also be the effect of hearing a different world view.

To manage conflict within our field we need to:
- understand the different responses to conflict
- create our own list of what is and what isn't acceptable
- ensure organisational support and a course of action.

Our individual responses to conflict are believed to be formed during childhood in response to our environment and our caregivers. Unless we've done a lot of work on ourselves or are approaching the conversation from a very relaxed state (why I like engaging farmers markets, see Chapter 6), our responses are going to be fairly automatic.

From a more schooled perspective, we can look at these response types from: **Fight, Flight, Freeze** and **Fawn**:

- **Fight trauma response** during conflict includes confrontation, rage and intense angry behaviours, while milder responses might include raised voices, sighing, folded arms or hand movements.
- **Flight trauma response** during conflict includes anxiety, panic and avoidance, and heightened energy, while milder responses include not coming back from a break or not returning to future workshops.
- **Freeze trauma response** during conflict includes dissociation, individuals not fully understanding questions, asking to rehear the question or repetition and responding with 'I don't know', while a milder response might be speaking emotionlessly or with low energy.
- **Fawn trauma response** during conflict includes deferring to others' needs, trying to appease perceived threats and displaying co-dependency.

While managing an individual experiencing a Fawn or Fight response might seem easier, if not detected, the consequences can be just as damaging as managing someone experiencing a Flight response.

Depending on the organisation and your role, you may have flexibility to consider the behaviours you regard reasonable or unreasonable and create your own set of boundaries, or you may need to adopt or negotiate the boundaries set within an organisation. When working with the public, we need to have a clear emotional slate and create (when calm and relaxed) our own set of boundaries, what we are comfortable and not comfortable accepting.

The following is my personal list of what I consider reasonable behaviours and unreasonable behaviours.

Reasonable behaviour	Unreasonable behaviour
Reasonable behaviour that does not compromise the health, safety, wellbeing and security of our people, other service users or the participants themselves. Some examples of reasonable behaviours include: • signs of frustration, rolling eyes, sighing or being unresponsive • adding emphasis with hand gestures and body language – hands on hips, crossing arms, waving hands around or finger pointing • changes in tone, including raised voice, fast speech or slow speech • threats to escalate complaints to other officers, councillors and the media.	Unreasonable behaviour is conduct that is unreasonable in all circumstances because it compromises the health, safety, wellbeing and security of our people, other service users or participants themselves. Some examples of unreasonable behaviours include: • acts of aggression, verbal abuse and derogatory, racist or grossly defamatory remarks • harassment, intimidation or physical violence • rude, confronting and/or threatening face-to-face or phone contact or correspondence • threats of harm to self or third parties, threats with a weapon or threats to damage property, including bomb threats • stalking (in person or online) • emotional manipulation.

It is important for you to have some tricks and self-care actions you can take in the face of escalating reasonable behaviours.

Here are my team's suggestions:
- Remove yourself from the situation with a common non-threatening excuse. Start the sentence with *Sorry*, then the action, then the reason (this is called **Breaking State**).
  - 'I'm sorry, I really need to go to the toilet, as I haven't been all day. It's been so busy. Give me two minutes.'
  - 'I'm sorry, this is not my area of expertise. My colleague knows much more about this topic. I will go and fetch them.'
- Focus in on your breathing while in the conversation. Focusing on three breaths (it's only six seconds) will bring you back to focus.
- Take a pause.
  - 'Do you mind if we take a quick pause or break? I understand this is a really important matter/concern for you. I am feeling a little out of my depth with this conversation. Can I grab a colleague?'

To manage conflict, it is important to find out or co-create a procedure that outlines what you will do in the event that behaviours at a pop up, workshop, town hall meeting cross into the unreasonable territory and what your organisation will support you with. Within Conversation Co, we call it the traffic light system – working through the steps to actively reduce and negotiate the unreasonable behaviour. We do find that **most** of the time, taking the first step and stating your boundaries and declaring you are feeling uncomfortable is enough to bring people back into line and have a breakthrough where they realise they need to self-manage.

Here is our system:
- State that you are feeling uncomfortable and the conversation will cease if the behaviour continues. For example:
  - 'I understand this is having a real impact on your life. I want to keep talking to you about this project; however, I need you to alter the tone in which you are talking to me.'
  - 'Why don't you take a moment. Can I get you a cup of tea?'
- If the person is still persisting and abusive, be clear the conversation has finished.
- Relocate engagement activities away from people exhibiting aggressive behaviour.
- If available, request security to remove the person/s exhibiting aggressive behaviour.
- Pack up and leave community engagement activities (regardless of the agreed or promoted engagement times).
- If unable to pack up safely, immediately leave or find a safe place (nearby cafe, vehicle) and call 000 to request police presence.

Here are our non-negotiables to create a safe working environment:
- Work in pairs (either with a client or another staff member).
- Maintain visibility of the other person, especially when undertaking intercepting. Be not farther than 50 metres from each other.

There are strategies to create psychological safety across this book and strategies to support people to bring their best selves.
- Chapter 2: Understanding the purpose of the engagement. Sometimes we are there to challenge, other times we are there to collect unfiltered ideas and aspirations.

- Chapters 6 and 7: Making sure your planning is on point (level of influence, method selection, staffing mix, level of information).
- Chapter 8: Getting the staffing mix right (having a mix of technical experts and people whisperers) along with any location-specific experts (e.g., local projects, events or happenings in the immediate pop up area).
- Chapter 12: Communicating what and where things are happening.

Did you know that you cannot eat and be angry at the same time? It is also why many of us stress eat – to induce those feelings of relaxation. The **parasympathetic nervous system (PSNS)**, sometimes called the rest and digest system, is part of the autonomic nervous system. Located between the brain and spinal cord, the PSNS is tasked with saving the body's energy by slowing the heart rate and increasing the activity of the intestines and glands during periods of rest. So, a well-fed group will be a more relaxed group. Catering is a good strategy for mildly hostile situations.

Getting the enthusiasm to the right level

Passionate people make the best conversationalists. Without interest or passion, participants are likely going to be apathetic towards the organisation or the project. There is an optimum level of 'enthusiasm' where we can converse.

In his model, Reframing Conflict, Peter Condliffe discusses how conflict, when managed well, can contribute towards better relationships, strategy and policy. Personally, I find apathy harder to deal with, and in Chapter 12 we look at generating interest.

Here are ways to get conflict to the appropriate model:

- Start where the person is at. Let their passion guide your starting point in the conversation (even if it's different to the topic of conversation). Think about your own reactions and what you do when you want something solved. You can visibly manage these off-topic conversations by capturing it.
  - o Have a separate sheet or form for different requests (Customer Service Request form if a follow-up is needed).
  - o Connect their interest to an area (if related to the consultation).
  - o Offer the opportunity to participate: 'I know you were here because of X. Since you are here, do you also want to provide some feedback on Y?'
- Open-ended questions are your friend. Avoid the word *Why* when asking follow-up questions. Instead, say 'Tell me more about that.'
- Accurate record-keeping lets people know you are taking what you are saying seriously and that their feedback will be included. Keep checking in on your understanding by reading out what you are writing or understanding.
- Name what you are feeling and state your boundaries. Work through your traffic light system above as needed.

It is also important to debrief and learn from each of our experiences, whether that be for future pop ups related to this project or delivering pop ups again in this community. In Chapter 10 we talk more about debriefing; however, it's important to share your experiences with others and seek support for difficulties experienced.

We have unpacked a lot in this first chapter. My intent is not to overwhelm you but rather empower you to design safety into the system you create within your organisation to safely deliver pop ups.

When working alongside technical experts, I regularly get asked, 'What if I am not confident in managing my boundaries?'

Working in the community is a skill like any other. It can take time to grow your muscle in this space. This is why we talk so much about getting the staffing mix right in Chapter 8. If you know the topic is likely to create lots of interest, be sure to work in closer proximity to each other. If you need to take a breather, try one of the ideas in this chapter to exit yourself (safely) from the conversation.

At a recent facilitator training session, I was asked by a person worried about offending a participant. We humans are funny; we all have boundaries, yet we aren't good at implementing them but support others that have them. It can feel difficult the first time you tell someone to tone down their language, but as long as you do it in a firm and reasonable way, you will be fine.

When you are back in the office, document and debrief the experience with your supervisor. Would you support someone who stated and firmly held their boundaries? Of course, you would, so trust that you will have the support of your manager. If not, go to their manager!

Take action

If you are going to take action on only one of the chapters within this book, please take action on this one.

1. If you're part of a larger team or organisation, reach out to your organisational performance team to understand if there is an agreed practice or policy to keep you and others safe in the community. If not, ask to be part of shaping it. Come up with your own definition of what is reasonable or unreasonable. When you are in a relaxed frame of mind, come up with your list of reasonable and unreasonable behaviours. Test it with others, get others to weigh in and see where you fit in.

2. Start a conversation within your team, or with your manager if in a larger organisation, about what your course of action is if the behaviours tip into the unreasonable territory.

3. Create a debriefing or incident report template that can be used to record incidents, actions and any learnings for next time. Go to www.conversationco.com.au/slpop to download cool resources.

In the next chapter, I talk about connecting pop ups back into your overall engagement program and how to schedule these to ensure maximum value from the interest generated.

Chapter 2

Connecting your pop up to your program

Pop ups can sometimes be considered the light-touch approach to engagement – a place where you can't generate the same discussion or cross-pollination of ideas that you can in a workshop, or where there is limited or no opportunity to educate the community on complex issues.

I obviously think differently about the value of pop ups and what they can bring to your engagement program when given half the chance with proper planning. Just like with any other engagement tool, you need to do as much planning to create that intentional conversation opportunity.

When planned well, pop ups can:
- significantly boost the number of people reached through your engagement

- connect to new audiences that may not have a strong connection with your organisation
- boost exposure and participation in other engagement methods
- provide greater visibility to the project – being **seen** on the street gives the sense your organisation cares and is making a genuine effort to engage
- build relationships by being face to face with the person behind the project. It helps to build relationships and demonstrate intentions of a decision, idea or proposal
- provide another touch point for your customers and your community to find out what else you can do, get support or get their immediate questions answered.

When not planned well, they can be a place where you spend two hours talking to the only person there – your colleague – about what you're planning for dinner, or they can be an experience where you face so much rejection – 'Not interested', 'No, thank you', 'Don't have time', 'Have to collect the kids', 'Running late', 'Just here to buy milk' – that you are counting down the clock and want the ground to open up and swallow you whole.

One of my favourite experiences was working with a transport planner – I promise all my stories aren't about transport planners. We were consulting on the preparation of an integrated transport plan for a large activity centre. I hadn't known at the time how nervous, and perhaps a little unconvinced, he was about doing pop ups in the community. We had done so much preparation, put effort into selecting the location (Chapter 6), had multilingual conversation facilitators, translated materials and lots of visual aids for conversations. He shadowed me a bit at the start. I did the awkward sales pitch (Chapter 12) – 'Have you got five minutes to talk about traffic/parking in …', did the spiel about what we were doing, guided them around and then gradually phased myself out, handing the conversation over to our friend.

Every time I checked in on him, he was deep in conversation, talking thoughtfully with someone, looking at maps, furiously taking notes. At the end of the first pop up, I remember him saying how much he enjoyed the session and the opportunity to talk to the general community about his findings and the proposed ideas and hear their insights and experiences about movement (car, bike and pedestrian) around the centre.

This experience is a great example of why we build in pop ups as part of our work. In this project, we engaged with very different people on the street to those who registered to attend, remembered the workshop date and came along to the workshop (think bicycle user group, rate payer association). Again, both have their value. It also gave the project lead the opportunity to sense-check their understanding, fill gaps in knowledge and compare what he had heard from some of the more organised groups to that of a layperson's view. I also see the joy these technical experts get when they share their project with others and when the person is interested.

In this chapter I will cover:
- Alignment of pop ups to your engagement plan: What can be achieved and the level of influence.
- Different styles of pop ups: Informational, conversational and how to plan and deliver each kind.
- Differences between a pop up and intercepts, and when to use either.
- When to schedule your pop ups within your engagement program for maximum value.

'Nothing in this world is worth having or worth doing unless it means effort, pain, difficulty.' Not sure if Theodore Roosevelt was describing the life of a community engagement practitioner; he got pretty close.

Align your pop ups to deliver your engagement plan

I am not going to recreate or reteach Planning Community Engagement 101; just as you have the overarching purpose for community engagement, these can be delivered through your pop up. Following are six examples from projects we have delivered using pop ups as a method.

The level of community influence is different across each project, and even within the project there might be different activities within one pop up that carry a different level of influence. We recently worked on a project where a local council was looking at upgrading a section of bike path (the project was going ahead – not a negotiable). During the pop up, we provided information about the project (inform only), collected community votes for the preferred option from three (Consult as Council would decide the final outcome) and also collected additional feedback from those voting for an option and those not supportive of the project overall (Consult as Council would finetune the final design).

Sample community engagement program purpose	Examples of how this can be achieved through your pop up
Share information about a new service or change to service	Introduction of food and organics service into the community – showing the new collection bin on display, the kitchen caddy, educating the community about what can and cannot go into this new bin.
Understand level of support or reactions to a proposal or idea	Test a master plan, a new idea or a series of options on display and show detail about the project. Seek feedback on the preferred option or elements of the idea. Seek out reasoning. Why/why not?
Create a change in behaviour	Create a climate change response plan and provide education and insights about the local context using a strengths-based approach to ask what participants are already doing in this space. Ask participants what, with support, would they like to do (e.g. install solar panels). Finally, ask participants to pledge a change they will make or practice they will adopt (e.g. take a reusable cup to a coffee shop).
Identify a problem or opportunity	Understand and improve safety within a particular area, including a walking tour that departs from your pop up and takes people around the area. Consider the varying spaces and where there are feelings of safety and unsafety.

Sample community engagement program purpose	Examples of how this can be achieved through your pop up
Social licence (achieving ongoing community acceptance or approval)	Planning scheme amendment for an area: Share the research undertaken and context, seek additional or missed information, share proposed objectives and actions and seek feedback. Explain the process for ongoing community involvement – submission process, panel process and publishing of outcomes along with the role of the body or organisation in the process.
Decision-making	Budgeting process with a set of pre-collected ideas, quick poll or voting card. Idea with the most unique votes is funded.

Aligning your engagement questions and making them pop up-specific is discussed more in Chapter 4: 'Make making sense easy'.

Plan for different pop ups

Not all pop ups are in a noisy main street with crowds of people talking; some are just off the beaten track, perhaps in a community room off the library with people on the footpath pulling you in (sometimes referred to as community drop-in). The type of pop up, the purpose and level of influence will determine the location (see Chapter 6 to choose an appropriate location to suit).

The most common pop up style is conversational – working with participants on an individual level, talking through the details of the project, taking on their feedback and answering their questions. This can be great when the topic is complex and the background information or context is challenging.

The other style is informational – provide a clear introduction and allow participants to explore the pop up stations in their own time and participate at their own pace. This can be great if the topic is more sensitive in nature and you want people to provide their honest opinion or views, free from reprimand.

Giving thought to how participants can have a completely self-guided experience, even if you plan on running a conversational-style pop up, will allow you to reach more people, especially during peak times. You don't want the number of people you can reach to be limited to the number of people you have staffing a pop up. For example, two staff speaking to each person for 10 minutes each over a two-hour pop up is capped at 24 people.

Here is how to set up for a self-guided/informational experience:
- Have a clear entry point with background information clearly labelled 'Start Here'. This can be a decal on the floor, a hand sanitiser station or some other form of welcome.
- Space out the questions and information, and start with some of the easier questions first; treat it like a first date. What question would you ask first to build into the big one?
- Knowledge-build – give enough information to answer the question and leave room for participants to seek out more if needed. You can use a QR code that connects

people back to a website or a handout that has links for more information.

- Have staff dotted throughout or dedicated to support people in each of these zones.
- Create a direction you want people to take or follow. This could be with arrows, having information beside or on the back of other information stands.
- Have a clear exit and explanation of next steps with any follow-up action you want people to take.

Pop up or intercept

The key difference between a pop up and an intercept is that the exact time and location of pop ups are promoted. With an intercept, you might give a general warning like 'We will be in Smiths Beach township over the next week, speaking to visitors, business owners and the general community about the project.' and that is it. The biggest advantage of a pop up is having a range of activities to suit the varying levels of interest and time someone has available, compared to an intercept where you usually have one activity – survey or voting card.

Here is a side-by-side look at the differences between an intercept and a pop up:

Item	Pop Up	Intercept
Benefit	More opportunities to provide feedback (more than one activity). Good visibility. People come prepared. Create interest and excitement from people gathering. Increased safety for staff. Environmental risks are managed better (access, weather).	More mobile; can get into different areas more easily. More locations are happy to support this style with minimum set-up. More cost effective (less set-up time, no booking fees). Really getting to the average person. Can cancel easily (rain) or change location if something happens on the site plan.

Item	Pop Up	Intercept
Constraint	People can avoid you (cross the road to avoid visiting that section of street/area). More restrictions from venues about set-up style and access requirements. Less locations can be visited on the one day because of set-up requirements. Need to stick to the site and time, even if it's not ideal once you arrive. People have to find you; if they can't, they can get angry.	People can feel unprepared to engage (limited notice of your approach). People can feel pressured into participating. Increased risk to staff, as they might be moving to locations out of site. Increased movement of staff (accessibility and fitness might be a concern). Less visible if the project being seen is a priority. Tougher on staff – cold approach.
Set-up	More set-up designed to create a presence in the area (display boards, caravan, larger props)	Minimal set-up designed to be on the move (iPads, maybe a banner and your team)

Item	Pop Up	Intercept
Time	>2 hours in the one location	<90 minutes in the one location
Activities	Can have multiple stations – information, voting, detailed questions	Single activity – usually a quick survey or quick poll
Time with person	5 to 20 minutes	<5 minutes

When to schedule your pop ups for maximum value

This is not a self-criticism or a criticism of any of my clients; I've not had an engagement program launch when we thought it would launch, whether it's the kick-off or the date written in the tender. Despite the best efforts of all involved, something holds us back – waiting on an approval, getting some further information, or something controversial happening in the community.

Pop ups or any face-to-face engagement are often the most costly method to deliver. You really want to get the maximum value out of them so that through the exposure you:
- promote the project in general
- draw people back into the other engagement methods (survey, workshop registration)
- others share it with their networks, friends and family.

Following is my project launch sequence for a four-week campaign with four pop ups:

Day 0: Soft launch online. Don't launch on a Friday; rather, launch on a Wednesday so you can monitor feedback and involvement during business hours. See how your community or customers are responding to it. If there are any polarising comments or questions, you can respond fast, unless you have the team available to help answer or solve those solutions over the weekend.

Day 1 to 4: Monitor and adjust. After the information has begun trickling out to the community, all the **keenly interested** people have tested your platform and questions. You can see if you need to make any tweaks to your messaging or questions if you are getting vastly different responses to what you hoped for.

Day 5 to 21: First, second and third pop up. Hold your pop up within the first week. This can help you to attract or invite attendees to other events. After each pop up, we notice a spike in online engagement, extra survey responses, more project views or registrations for a panel or workshop.

Day 21: Schedule your workshops. Having a workshop in your engagement campaign gives those interested and impacted the best opportunity to find out about the project, time to forget about it, see it again and register.

Day 22 to 25: Final pop up. Hold the final pop up with two days (minimum) remaining in the consultation period to give people a chance to complete a survey or find out more information about the project. If you hold all of the pop ups in the first couple of weeks, people get really annoyed that they missed the opportunity to speak with someone in person. If you hold it too late, then you miss the spike in online participation. If your consultation closes on a Sunday and hold the pop up the same day, people going back to their offices on a Monday and try logging on to complete a survey will find it closed.

Following this sequence will give you maximum value from those pop ups.

My topic is just too complex

You might find yourself still trying to convince project leads to include a pop up, I imagine you'll get told, 'My project is just too complex for a pop up. I think a town hall meeting would be best.'

Say this: 'I absolutely agree with you. We need to use a mixed methods approach, as each tool has its advantages and disadvantages. Just like using an online survey doesn't allow participants to ask questions or see what others are thinking or writing, we will only have a short time (5 to 10 minutes) to spend with really interested and engaged people.

'We can, though, get their details and offer to speak to them outside of the pop up at another time. We can also have as much information about the project available so they can do their own research, and then encourage them to go home and do the online survey if they think of anything else. For the majority of the people we speak to at the pop up, this might be the only time they engage with us or this project and we have the chance to talk to them. So, what day and where do you think we should hold our first pop up?'

I want other participants to see what others say

Another common concern from project leads can be that using a pop up means ideas are static and not shared. This is not a method issue, it's a design adjustment. Personally, I don't love dotmocracy questions when used to decide on an eventual outcome. I like using them when it's about preferences, needs or interests – because it can be powerful to see what others in the community are after. I just would be careful about creating groupthink.

Another consideration needs to be privacy. If the conversation is more topical and likely to create a divide, you want to consider how to protect the identity of the people participating. If people are signing up for a workshop, they have a choice whether to speak or hold their opinions and ideas close to their chest. If people are writing out their ideas, you can have a pin board and pin up ideas and feedback. Have people write directly onto a board or a Post-it note that gets pinned up.

Take action

If you are an internal community engagement advisor, consider writing up your launch sequence to share with other project leads, or you can download a sample launch sequence at www.conversationco.com.au/slpop.

In the next chapter, I talk about how to make sure pop ups can be relevant to all of your stakeholders and what tiny touches you can make to attract or accidentally deter some stakeholders from participating.

Chapter 3

Pop ups can be for everyone

When talking to our clients about adding a pop up into their engagement program, a common objection is that their person of interest is not going to come to a pop up.

It is important to recognise the difference in engagement between being 'open to everyone' and being 'safe, welcoming and inclusive for everyone'. We need to recognise and design out the barriers that some individuals and groups may face when being a part of the conversation. By doing your research, mapping your stakeholders and creating a targeted approach, you can remove some barriers, provide support and actively target communities.

'You've cherry-picked what you are showing the community. This will skew the results.'

'I agree it looks like that. We've selected a few questions from the survey to encourage those with less knowledge than yourself to have a say and, hopefully, as a result of today, find out more.'

This was the conversation I had with a resident of a very controversial sporting project. This person wasn't the target stakeholder for the pop up. They had participated in an interview and attended many of the workshops, and we were using pop ups as a tool to speak to other park and reserve users. We visited the park before work to speak with dog walkers and morning athletes, visited on game day to speak with families and existing sporting users, visited on non-game days to get the recreational users, and visited a nearby shopping strip to speak to nearby residents we probably hadn't spoken to yet who use the park on occasion. We needed to make a few more changes outside of our timing to ensure the project in this example benefited from a wider sample of stakeholder groups and individuals.

When you design and deliver pop ups in a safe and inclusive manner, you build integrity in your process, attract a wider audience and hear the diverse views of a larger sample size. These are the more obvious benefits of inclusive engagement, but there are a few hidden benefits.

Improving relationships within your community. We've had participants share that they were unsure how similar their views were to that of a different person, race and age, learnt something new about a particular group or had their ideas challenged.

Making participation a cultural norm, providing feedback to the government and sharing ideas is not a typical process for everyone. It can encourage ongoing dialogue and involvement in the process and project through the gesture of an invitation.

- Bringing visibility to different stakeholder groups and individuals interested in a project or living in an area. We once ran a Changing Faces Campaign about development in the area to bring visibility to who was moving into the area, their interests and their needs to increase relatability and acceptance for the project.
- Advocating to project leads, leaders and your network for services, locations and times that will make your engagement activities more accessible (and therefore effective).

Not having a representative consultation/engagement with the community may lead to:

- communities becoming disenfranchised and not seeing themselves as part of the project/process that our client is undertaking
- people losing trust in the client and/or the process
- not gaining the insights or outcomes desired from the project, including a diversity of voices.

Accessibility and inclusion benefit everyone, and the goal of this chapter is to make improvements in how you consider the needs of your stakeholders.

14 ways to create access and inclusion across your engagement program:

1. Don't make assumptions.
2. Use plain English, images and diagrams in print and socials.
3. Use and accept a variety of communication tools – online and print surveys; telephone conversations; Zoom meetings; in-person meetings; written, video, audio and LOTE (Languages Other Than English) documents and submissions.
4. Preference-free events and gatherings.
5. Ensure physical accessibility.
6. Deliver pop ups at different times and locations.
7. Provide engagement activities for children to support participation.
8. Ask people how they identify and what words/language they prefer to use.
9. Ask individuals what support is needed or how you can support their participation in the engagement activity.
10. Take the time to build rapport and trust.
11. Acknowledge people's contribution – verbally, written thank you letters, and remuneration where appropriate.
12. Be prepared to shut down discriminatory comments or offensive behaviour.
13. Wear badges that show you are an ally and your pronouns to encourage others to follow suit.
14. When designing project documentation, use contrasting colours to assist users with vision impairments and display important sections to differentiate areas that need to stand out.

In this chapter you will learn to consider the barriers different people face and try to lower those barriers in the planning process and throughout the engagement.

Considering the needs of your stakeholders starts way back in the engagement planning phase of your project. Three traditional forms of stakeholder mapping are:
- Mapping interest and impact: Consider the level of interest and/or impact the project has on stakeholders.
- Mapping the relationship to your organisation: How do these groups of individuals interact with your organisation? Are they active, do they sit back and watch what is happening, or are they partners in your work?
- Mapping physical location or connection: For place-based projects, consider the needs of stakeholders by their physical location or connection to the project (adjacent residents, living within 500 metres, transit through the area).

The following considerations have been sectioned into different identities or roles that people may have. It is essential to recognise that people are never just one thing. To consider the barriers different people face, you need to think about the different aspects of a person's identity that can expose them to overlapping forms of discrimination and marginalisation. This is known as **intersectionality**, and it acknowledges that everyone has their own unique experiences of discrimination and oppression, and we must consider everything and anything that can marginalise people.

An example of intersectionality may be a woman with caring responsibilities whose first language is Mandarin. The main barrier to participation for this person is her responsibilities as a carer, as she has excellent English language skills.

First Peoples

Reference is given to two distinct cultural groups made up of Aboriginal and Torres Strait Islander peoples. In reality, there are over 250 different language groups spread across Australia. Along with different language groups, there are distinct groups each with their own culture, customs, languages and laws.

Actions we can take in our work to support participation

- Participants may purposely or inadvertently express views that are disrespectful and inaccurate to and about First Peoples. To set expectations of respect and inclusion, it is important to have tools that enable you to shut down racist or biased comments such as 'That's an interesting view, Bob; however, research in this area shows xyz.'
- Where possible, use co-design to develop the engagement initiatives, sites and times to enable maximum participation from the community.
- Go where First Peoples are. See if you can attend Local Aboriginal Network meetings, Aboriginal gathering place events or other community meetings.
- When engaging with Aboriginal organisations and Traditional Owners, explore the expectations of compensation for their time and include them within project budgets.
- Allow audio and visual contributions.
- At pop ups and events, wear an Aboriginal and Torres Strait Islander badge, signalling to people that they are safe with you.
- Consider outsourcing this component of engagement to agencies that specialise in engaging with Aboriginal and Torres Strait Islanders.

People with disability and chronic health issues

Disability is when a person's body structure, activity or participation is significantly impaired by a health condition. This can include conditions caused by accidents, illness, genetic disorders, ageing or injury. Many disabilities are not visible, and not all people with significant impairment by a health condition identify as a person with disability.

One in six Australians (18%) identify as a person with disability. An additional 22% have long-term health conditions, and the remaining 60% do not have either.

Over three-quarters (76.8%) of people with disabilities reported a physical disorder as their main condition. The most common physical disorder was musculoskeletal disorder (29.6%) including arthritis and related disorders (12.7%) and back problems (12.6%).

Actions we can take in our work to support participation
- Ask participants how we can make it easier for them to participate and include this feedback in continuous improvement.
- Use available budgets to support specific disability-support services, such as an Auslan interpreter or scribe.
- Provide seating or position engagement activities near public seating.
- Provide opportunities for reading or talking through materials and scribing for participants.
- Clear and consistent signage at events and in-person workshops.
- Use size 12 font or larger in documents.
- Describe slides or visual aids when presenting to people with vision impairment.

People experiencing mental health challenges

Around 1 in 2 Australians aged 16 to 85 have experienced a mental health issue at some point in their lifetime, with around 1 in 5 of the same cohort having experienced a mental issue in the previous 12 months.

There are particular types of mental health challenges that may pose barriers for engagement, such as social phobia. Social phobia affects around 3% of Australians during any given year. Situations that require the demonstration of social skills, such as having conversations and participating in group work, are more challenging for those experiencing social phobia.

Actions we can take in our work to support participation

- Locate activities close to communities so that travel is easy and locations are familiar.
- Ensure a mixture of engagement methods, including online, in-person, written and digital.
- Provide detailed information about the engagement activity online or where it is promoted, expectations, intended outcomes and processes.
- Have a clear structure and journey for the engagement; clutter can divide attention.
- Be patient. People may need time to warm up to activities or think of responses.
- Continued contact. If your pop up usually requires you to hand over a person to the next officer, consider continue taking the person through the entire activity yourself.
- Provide opportunities for participants to ask questions privately to avoid embarrassment.

- Provide opportunities for reading or talking through materials and scribing for participants.
- Provide clear and consistent signage at events and in-person workshops.

Socioeconomic status

Socioeconomic status encompasses not only income but also educational attainment, occupational prestige and subjective perceptions of social status and social class.

In community engagement, we need to recognise that participating in our projects can require significant time, travel, access to technology, levels of literacy and education, and confidence to participate.

Actions we can take in our work to support participation:
- Time activities to accommodate people who work various days and shifts or who have caring responsibilities.
- Host pop ups at free events and free locations.
- Locate activities close to communities so that travel is easy and affordable.
- Consider public transport routes and timetables when scheduling activities.
- Provide opportunities for participants to ask questions privately to avoid embarrassment.
- Don't assume that everyone can do what we are asking them to do. Always provide options (e.g. write your response or speak your response).
- Provide activities to keep children engaged while parents participate.

- Hire additional facilitators to work with people who require support to scribe, understand engagement materials, or provide more time to work through questions or activities.
- Provide meals to encourage participation and create a welcoming environment.

LGBTIQA+

Lesbian, gay, bisexual, trans and gender-diverse, intersex, queer and asexual (LGBTIQA+) communities included within this commonly-used term have distinct experiences and needs.

Dominant social and cultural assumptions about gender reinforce the idea that it is biologically predetermined and unchanging, but this fails to recognise and validate the ways that gender evolves and changes collectively over time and individually for many people. Binary and rigid gender norms also reinforce inequality for women and generate experiences of exclusion for anyone who does not fit stereotypical ideals of *masculine* and *feminine*.

Actions we can take in our work to support participation
- Identify significant dates such as awareness months and celebratory events, and plan engagement respectfully to work with or around these significant dates.
- Consider engaging with existing LGBTIQA+ groups or at planned LGBTIQA+ events.
- For some people, identifying as LGBTIQA+ during engagement may not feel or be safe for them. Plan the collection of this data in a way that provides ways for participants to share this without compromising their personal feeling of safety or fearing negative impacts of sharing this.

- At pop ups and events, wear an ally badge, signalling to LGBTIQA+ people that they are safe with you.
- Encourage the sharing of pronouns on name labels and when making introductions. Ask people what pronouns they use; don't assume.
- Use open questions that do not assume someone is heterosexual and cisgender (including on surveys, demographic collection, postcards, interviews, etc.).
- Use non-gendered descriptions that do not assume someone is heterosexual and cisgender – like parent/guardian/partner rather than mum/dad/wife.
- Demonstrate comfort when using LGBTIQA+ language. If you accidentally misgender someone, apologise, correct yourself and move on. For example, 'I think she was saying – sorry, I think **they** were saying ...'
- Be willing to let people represent their lives in their chosen terms.
- When designing gender questions, give people options like including 'Prefer not to say', 'Non-binary' and an 'Other' free text option for people to self-identify. If collecting contact information, allow people to provide a 'Preferred name' and alternative titles, like 'Mx' or 'No Titles'.

Culturally and linguistically diverse (CALD) communities

CALD is a bureaucratic term, and not an identity. It is used to describe the diverse populations and individuals that come from non-English speaking backgrounds. English-speaking people from New Zealand, the United Kingdom, Northern Ireland, Canada and the United States are not considered CALD. Despite there being some cultural differences, they do not face the same cultural and linguistic barriers people from other backgrounds experience.

CALD communities are not homogenous. We need to be mindful of diversity within communities and take an intersectional approach. It could be argued that this term is problematic, as it assumes that white Anglo language and culture as the 'norm' and everything else as different. It is important to recognise that people from white English-speaking backgrounds experience privilege in Australia, and despite the CALD term being questionable, it does acknowledge the work required to reduce barriers for people from non-Anglo backgrounds.

People from CALD communities may:
- be cautious about government and authority
- have a lack of knowledge of Australian processes, politics and such
- use different body language and eye contact
- use social hierarchy, like elders speaking on behalf of the community
- have different gender roles – e.g. it may not be permissible for a man and a woman (not from the same family) to be alone in a room together, or non-family members may not touch one another (pat on the shoulder and the like)
- experience language and literacy barriers
- be worried about being misunderstood or becoming embarrassed
- lack access to technology.

New arrivals to Australia may not have the time or access to resources to participate in engagement activities due to the fact that establishing themselves in a new country takes considerable physical and emotional energy.

Actions we can take in our work to support participation
- Building relationships and gaining trust is key to meaningful engagement with CALD communities.
- Where possible, use co-design to develop engagement initiatives, sites and times to enable maximum participation from the community.
- Consider engaging with CALD groups or at planned events.
- Produce collateral materials/socials in the languages of the main or target CALD communities of the region.
- Employ interpreters for workshops and events.
- Encourage other language contributions as well as audio and visual contributions.
- Engage conversation facilitators versed in multiple languages to assist with participation.

Home life/family/living arrangements

People across our communities have many different living arrangements. We need to think carefully about how we design our engagement tools to enable participation for people with different arrangements and to be inclusive with our language. People with caregiving responsibilities may experience barriers to being involved with projects and programs.
- There are ways we can phrase our questions to be more inclusive and may provide richer and more nuanced data.
- People who are experiencing homelessness or housing insecurity may not have the emotional capacity to participate in engagement activities.

- Standard questions may unintentionally make people feel uncomfortable; asking people where a person lives may be jarring for a person experiencing housing insecurity.
- People who have caregiving responsibilities may be time-poor and/or have different availability to other cohorts.
- People who live on their own may experience social isolation and lack confidence to be part of community events and activities.

Actions we can take in our work to support participation
- Plan engagement activities for different times of day, both in-person and online (if possible).
- Offer childcare or respite options for in-person workshops.
- Go where caregivers are. Plan your pop ups near playgrounds and schools, outside community centres and libraries.
- Avoid falling back on broad terminology, such as *families*, in engagement questions that make assumptions about everyone having a family. This may exclude community members.
- Use sensitivity when using terms such as *parent*, which may inadvertently exclude non-familial or non-parental guardians of children – use *parent/guardian* where possible.
- Provide colouring-in stations and toys at in-person workshops and pop ups.
- Consider accessibility for people using mobility devices, prams and pushers.
- For surveys or pop ups, consider asking broader demographic questions such as 'What suburb do you usually spend your time in?' rather than 'Where do you live?'.

Age and life stages

People experience different barriers and enablers for participation at different stages of their lives.

- Children often have little to no input in engagement processes.
- Prejudice against young people being difficult or lazy can be a barrier.
- Young adults may be hard to engage with and need a clear reason or 'hook'.
- Middle-aged people may be time-poor, with full work and caregiving load.
- Ageism – older people are perceived to be less 'with it'.
- Older people are more likely to be socially isolated.
- Older people experience higher rates of visual and hearing impairment.

Actions we can take in our work to support participation

- Consider the physical access for frail and vulnerable people in attending pop ups, workshops and events, and have seating available.
- Consider engaging with ageing well or positive ageing groups or at planned seniors' events.
- Consider bringing along seats for older people to comfortably engage.
- Foster positive attitudes of older people and young people.
- Use large text for presentations and documents.
- Bear in mind older people are more likely to be socially isolated – you may be the first person to speak to them in days; allow additional time for a chat.
- Provide a private space for participation, particularly for

young people, if you are seeking feedback on something sensitive in nature.

- Provide incentives like a voucher for a yoghurt, a hot beverage or snacks onsite. This can help increase participation, particularly among young people.
- Don't assume digital literacy or access to technology.
- Use venues that have audio loops to assist those who require hearing assistance.

Neurodiversity

Neurodiversity is the concept that all humans vary in terms of neurocognition. The term neurodiversity recognises the unique strengths and challenges that may derive from thinking, learning and communicating differently.

Neurodiversity isn't the same thing as disability, though people who have neurodivergent features may need accommodations at work or school. Types of neurodivergent conditions include dyslexia, dyspraxia, autism, ADHD and Tourette syndrome. Being neurodivergent may bring exceptional skills and talents such as innovation, creativity and problem-solving.

Actions we can take in our work to support participation
- Have a clear structure and journey for the engagement; clutter can divide attention.
- Key information should be contrasted with non-essential information.
- Use plain language and avoid jargon.
- Use questions that can be answered literally and are not ambiguous.

- Provide detailed information about the engagement activity, expectations, intended outcomes and processes. Consider developing a social script.
- Make sure directions are clear, with a picture if possible, and have clear wayfinding.
- Too much information can cause confusion and stress. Avoid distracting backgrounds and large blocks of text.
- Some people will take all that you say literally. Consider how information is presented.
- Give participants a choice in how they engage – in how they contact you (phone or email), in how they access and provide information (paper, online, video, audio) and when. Some people need to go away and think about it before they respond.
- Some people will not like being approached. They may want to scan a QR code and walk away.
- Avoid physical contact.

I can imagine your mind, though opened, might be very full after this chapter. Your biggest concern (if you are anything like me) might be offending someone. We are all learning, and the biggest takeaway from this, particularly when in person, is to ask the individual what support they need to participate. If you make a mistake or slip up with your language, acknowledge it and move on.

Knowing what you know now, you might feel that it's even harder to deliver in-person engagement. Start with our top 14 tips at the start of the chapter. Get those right and then build from there. Remember to reach out to other agencies and groups that support or provide services to the target group of interest, and ask their advice.

Take action

If you are in Australia or New Zealand, look up your community profile in profile.id. While you can't look up all the groups presented, you can find out the spread of ages, household structure, and place of birth along with education and need for assistance.

Consider creating a list of organisations that support these target groups and finding out if anyone in your organisation has an existing relationship. Otherwise, it might be time you connected.

In the next chapter, I help you consider how to capture data from your pop ups to ensure it can be analysed within your broad engagement report.

Chapter 4

Make making sense easy

Like the rest of my engagement colleagues, I love a good Post-it note – it's bright, inexpensive and very tactile. Sometimes those pesky Post-it notes have a mind of their own on windy days, and as was the case with a recent project (where the community was quite outraged), said Post-it notes went flying across the road, causing our community members to become angry with our 'unprofessional and blatant disregard' for their feedback. Not the best first impression.

Over the years we have explored other collection tools that still give you that bright and tactile feel, yet allow for better integration into the rest of the data set you've collected. I will talk you through how to plan for and integrate your pop up data into the rest of your data.

I trust that by now you're convinced that pop ups play an important role in boosting participation numbers and reaching those harder-to-reach audiences. But, if the data is not collected properly, this wisdom may not carry the same weight as other data sources – surveys, interviews – particularly when the data collected is asked in a different manner or without demographic details.

The benefits of collecting and integrating your pop up data into your main data set are:

- larger sample size from where you can draw more information
- larger subgroup sample and analysis, especially from those harder to reach
- greater confidence in the engagement findings, as you are drawing meaning from a complete set.
- life of the data is extended, as other projects can use the data where there is a topic or stakeholder crossover.

We've seen decision-makers disregard feedback when they are unsure of how it was collected – who said what and where the information came from – particularly, projects that are more controversial in nature. Don't let your countless hours of pounding the pavement or eating cinnamon donuts at markets go to waste. It's your job to make sure the wisdom shared by participants gets to where it needs to be.

Pop ups, as a tool, give you a better opportunity to ask questions and then observe behaviours and reactions, so it's in your interest to change the way you approach data collection. In this chapter you will learn:

- what questions to prioritise when you are out in the community
- barriers to collecting feedback and how to overcome this
- how to tweak your engagement questions so you don't sound like a robot

- how to avoid data collection mistakes that will take you hours to fix.

Again, another confession: Data collection and analysis were (are, maybe) not my strong point. I've been fortunate to work with some brilliant minds who can pull together various streams of data, code, analyse it and weave it into a story.

Early on in projects, we were analysing activities separately (you still might be doing this; don't worry we've got you). The difficulty in analysing data this way is that it doesn't give you a sense of the themes across the consultation and the key issues or commonalities across stakeholders or participants. I wasn't linking data very well; rather, I was using our pop up data more as a popularity contest to show the number of participants we spoke with. Back in the day, we weren't linking data back to demographics, making it impossible to do any analysis greater than themes (cross-tabulation, reporting by cohort).

Changing our approach meant that we can now report on data collected with so much more accuracy. Meaning, our pop up data has as much integrity and weight as other data sources.

Here is how you can make 'making sense' easy when it comes to data collected through pop ups:

Anchor pop up data to the survey

Start by writing the survey for the project. In our company, once the survey is approved by our client, we pull out up to four questions that either are more exploratory in nature or would benefit from seeking more detail from participants in person or watching the reactions to their responses.

Personalise or de-identify the way you ask the question

When writing survey questions, you might use more filler words or provide more explanation to help the person provide feedback. At a pop up, however, there is an opportunity for the person to seek clarity from a project member or from further information; similarly, you can also extract more information from the participant.

Surveys provide participants with a confidential tool to provide their response, so there may be a need to alter the way you ask a question to allow for a de-identified response or think through the layout of your pop up for privacy.

Following are some examples of how we've tweaked our base questions to be more in-person-friendly.

Base question example	In-person-friendly
Which of these situations make older people feel more lonely? (multiple choice)	What are five situations that might make older people feel isolated or lonely? (free text)
Do you feel that ___ customer service has improved over the last four years? (multiple choice, free text)	How can ____ improve its customer service? (free text)

How concerned are you that we will experience climate change, extreme weather events or natural disasters in the future that could affect the water supply? (Likert scale) Then, (conditional): 1.1. Are you satisfied that xxx are taking steps to plan for any future events? (Y/N/Not sure) 1.2. What are you most concerned could happen in the future? (open)	How would you like xxx to prepare for climate change or natural disasters in the future? (free text)

Use the same question type

An easy fix to better align your pop up data is asking the question at the pop up in the same manner you ask it within the survey (or workshop). For example, don't change a checkbox question to an open-ended question unless it has an 'Other' option, or don't change the number of responses required from 'top three' to 'top five'.

Bring the question to life; make it age-friendly

With an understanding of your participants and stakeholders from Chapter 3, use a range of data collection tools that provide both an interesting and interactive experience for participants while giving the project teams the information they need for their projects.

Here are our favourite five ideas for collecting data, use and any limitations.

Tool	Use	Limitations
Postcard	Allows participants to roam the pop up and record responses in one collection tool. Allows participants to provide confidential feedback. This can be linked to their demographic details for better segment reporting.	Smaller amounts of space for writing ideas as general A5 size (double sided). Intensive write-up if experiencing high volumes of participation.
Worksheet	Encourages creative thinking by including an opportunity to draw or describe their response. This can be linked to their demographic details for better segment reporting.	Person analysing a worksheet may need to make assumptions about what the participant has drawn and the meaning behind this. Intensive write-up if experiencing high volumes of participation.

Tool	Use	Limitations
Poster boards	Great for collecting short responses to a question or idea. Can be collected directly from the board or via a Post-it note. Provides other participants an entry point to discussions, opportunity to review what others think and expand on others' ideas.	Can lead to groupthink. Results need to be recorded and are not generally linked to demographic information.
Voting/ Dotmocracy	Great for sharing people's views in a quick, visual manner. Can be accompanied by images or maps for participants to add a spatial element to their vote.	Can lead to groupthink. Results need to be recorded and are not generally linked to demographic information.
Shortened Survey	Can provide an opportunity to complete key survey questions in an accessible format. Provide the number of questions that can be completed in the time available (7 minutes).	Can reduce the chance of participants completing the full survey.

Tool	Use	Limitations
Recorded interview	Useful when accompanying a worksheet or children's drawing. By having the participant talk through their design, vision or drawing, you get more detail and insights.	Intensive to code and theme, particularly if dealing with multiple participants. Best to use with a transcribing service like Otter AI to reduce transcribing time. Will need to allow time to clean up the data.

Use a mix of activities

These activities work well together. By selecting a few different approaches, you can reach a variety of participants across age and interest. Also accommodate for the time that participants might have to spend answering questions.

Consider how much demographic detail or personal information you need

We worked on a project that involved three separate organisations. Each organisation had different requirements around the collection of demographic and personal information. Organisations 1 and 2 had simple demographic collection requirements, while Organisation 3 required participants to provide their name, email address and responses to demographic questions prior to participating. Differences in participation numbers were huge, despite similar promotional levels, number of pop up events and question length/time to participate.
- Organisation 1: 702 participants
- Organisation 2: 767 participants
- Organisation 3: 157 participants

It can feel like a wasted opportunity not asking participants to complete demographic identifiers, or you can feel that there is a risk of duplication in responses. However, the premise of a pop up is speaking with people as they go about living life in their community, unlike a survey where they have actively paused their life to put time and energy into providing their feedback. The more time you spend asking participants about themselves, the less time is available to answer project questions.

Store the data for easy collation

Have a plan for how you are going to store data collected from each pop up. After a day in the field, it can be easy to mentally check out, and leaving the task to your later self isn't as simple as it seems. Depending on what and how your data is collected on the day, you could be left with a stack of feedback to many different questions. It is important to walk in with a plan, whether it be plastic sleeves for loose notes, a container for demographic cards (and for privacy) or even a handy rubber band to keep things separated. If you are planning to head off to another engagement session shortly after, **always** make a note of where this data came from and take the pressure off your memory.

Whether you or someone else on the team is handling the write-up, it's important that you carry on this organisation when you get back to the office.

A couple of things you could ask yourself now are:
- Is it easy to tell where this information came from?
- Have I labelled which questions the feedback responds to?

What you do back in the office matters too

Set up a spreadsheet that combines data from multiple sources. Start with whatever engagement tool has the most questions and/or the most complex questions. This will usually be your survey. Label the first few columns with:
- **Data Source:** Which method the data came from.
- **Notes:** Particularly useful if you are coding this with someone else.
- **Response ID:** Many online tools and surveys give you an automatic response ID. Ensuring data is connected to an ID helps when you are doing staged data downloads from an online tool. You can check that you have all data and reduce the likelihood of duplication.

Label the remaining columns with the questions from the engagement method with the most and/or complex questions including open, closed and demographic questions. Expect this to be a very large spreadsheet. Try to follow the order that the questions appear in this engagement method; if using your survey as your basis and the demographic questions are at the end of the survey, have these questions in the later columns to make exporting data easier.

Next, put rows at the top of the spreadsheet. Write the different sources the data is likely to come from, for example:
- community survey
- workshops
- pop ups
- email submissions.

Then, colour each row differently so you can keep track of what questions are asked in what technique, and you can write the word *Yes* in each column cell that relates to that question that is included in that method. For example, you might have asked two questions from the survey along with all of the demographic questions at your pop up, so in the row labelled pop up, there would be a *Yes* in the corresponding cells of the question columns. If you have reworded questions, you can type the question instead of typing the word *Yes* in the column. This will help you to remember the variation when it comes to analysis.

When it comes to entering data from your pop ups, Response ID will be the date or the pop up location, if important. You would then type in the comments collected under the corresponding questions, and if you collected demographics linked to the comments, you then enter these in the same row. If demographic data is not linked to comments, you may wish to create a separate spreadsheet that records responses to demographic questions.

I often hear from project teams, particularly when internal project teams are collecting the data (and are the same team that is using the data), that they **don't want to put too much pressure on staff** who are working at the pop up; rather, they will record it on their notebooks (yep, have had this!). My counterargument for this is: 'You then spend weeks chasing that data; they delay, as they want to "type it up for you", then run out of time and give you their handwritten notes, which you need to interpret. So, save yourself time and reduce the stress by providing a data collection tool.'"

Another one I hear is **I will just listen to it and then record a sense of what was said**. Without a guide, the notes that staff take will be biased towards what they are interested in, not the full intent of feedback received (We all do it – hone into the information relevant to our work and disregard the rest. It's our brain's way of saving capacity). Also, it gives you no capacity to quantify the responses, themes or for whom this is important.

I want everything to go back to the survey

In Chapter 2, we talk about activities within the pop up and the difference between an intercept and a pop up. We often have the full survey available for anyone super interested and who has about 15 minutes to spend, even though your survey might take someone seven minutes to complete on their own. This time doubles when you are reading out the question, discussing it and completing the answers. If this is your only data entry source, you will have facilitators tied up with one person for 15 minutes, so a two-hour pop up with two staff has you speaking with 16 people.

Pop ups provide exposure and promotion for your project. By giving them a sampler enough to interest them, you can then encourage them to participate in or sign up for other methods.

Take action

Sign up to Pinterest (if not already a member) and create a board for data collection inspiration. Search for worksheets, surveys and data and start collecting ideas for your future pop ups.

In the next chapter, we have a bit of fun with selecting the right location and why I love farmers markets so much (it's not just because of the baked goods).

Chapter 5

Selecting the right location

If only everyone went to the market, our job would be easy. There aren't enough free coffees that can make up for a bad location, and you can't talk to people who aren't there. Learn how to select the right location for the people you need to speak to.

Now, before you think 'I can skip over this chapter', let me share a story about a pop up that nearly ended in residents chaining themselves to trees.

We'd been contracted by an organisation to deliver their pop ups. They had completed all of the planning, booked all of the locations and managed all of the communications. The topic of our conversation was climate change adaptation and response.

A metro location, this location was prone to increased temperatures in summer (heat island effect), had reduced tree canopy coverage and increased density and clearing of land as a result of increased development. From our client briefing, we knew there was going to be interest and concern in this topic from local residents and community groups.

A week into the consultation, the project was going well – the pop ups were well-attended and the conversations were on topic and provided information the project team could use. However, it all went pear-shaped when we attended the next pop up – a community centre in a built-up area. The centre had a coffee shop that was popular among morning commuters. Our first hour was great. We spoke to residents on their way to work and lured them in with a free coffee. Then, two trucks arrived and began to cut down and chip up the two trees onsite. The works had been approved and scheduled, but the booking hadn't made it to the department in charge of this project. We then spent the next hour answering questions from residents furious about the project while listening to the rhythmic sounds of chainsaw and woodchipper as our backing track. You can imagine the type of feedback we received that day:

- Council approving the removal of trees for development.
- Council not notifying residents of the changes onsite.
- Concern the resident possum was going to be found and/ or relocated.
- Council's plans to replace these trees with others.

Our pop up also ended up on Facebook and in the local area's community newspaper, our climate change project signage in the foreground of a tree being cut down and chipped in the background. We also generated a lot of additional work for the Mayor's office in the form of resident letters and emails.

The location really does impact the success of your pop up. You can put all of your energy into nicely designed graphics, bring along your internal and external experts and even have a coffee van. However, if the location is disrupted because of roadworks or tree removal, or if the area is avoided because people feel unsafe, then be prepared to change your plans.

When you get the location right, you can:
- choose the location to infill likely gaps in your reach (children, young people, families and culturally diverse communities)
- match the project team to the location and likely topics of interest
- raise the profile and visibility of your project (without the media attention above)
- gain the views of the 'average' community member
- make it easy for people to participate as they go about their day.

In this chapter, I share how to:
- select a location and time suited to the person or people you want to engage with
- match the set-up to the location
- book a location and likely lead time needed.

Finding the people

Where are the people you want to speak to? The time you are at a location can drastically change who you will speak to and the mood or frame of mind of the participant when they come to speak to you. Think about your own movements and mood as you move around your community. When are you more open to speak to someone and when are you in head-down-hustle-in-and-get-out mode?

Being in a shopping centre might have come to mind. They can be a great place to speak to almost everyone and, at other times, no one. In Australia, the Age Pension is typically paid once a fortnight on a Thursday; being at a shopping centre on this day, usually during morning tea and lunch (10 am to 12 pm), is a great time to speak to older people. School holidays at shopping centres are also great for reaching families with children. After school, food courts and gaming locations can be great places to reach young people. Likewise, 5 pm on a Tuesday night is not a great time to speak to someone at the front of a supermarket. They might speak to you out of feelings of obligation or if they are super interested. However, they will be in a completely different mood than if you had spoken to them Sunday morning at a local farmers market. We've noticed people are more civically minded when they have the time and space to think.

Competing for attention

You have about eight seconds to grab someone's attention. The amount of effort you need to put into your set-up (covered in Chapter 10) changes based on the location. Sometimes the locations with the most people or captive audiences – festivals, agricultural shows, markets and even shopping centres – can be the toughest to compete for attention.

We were tasked with designing a pop up to talk to residents about the design and redevelopment of the pool. The only pop up for this project was attending the local agricultural show. We knew we'd be competing with other events and rides, food stall holders and other community organisations running free or low-cost activities, so we decided to create an interactive prop similar to that of a water dunking experience at an amusement park. People stood under it, and the operator released small rice-filled bean bags that hit them on the head and gave them a fright! While people were queuing up (yes, we had a line), we spoke to them about what we were doing, and once they finished scaring themselves, we moved them onto the other activities and boards.

The biggest compliment I heard that day was 'Is this activity free?'. If you can't compete despite the draw of a big crowd, you might be better off being in a smaller location and have less but more quality conversation.

We could not have had the same design and set-up if we were standing on the street in front of someone's shop. We would have blocked foot traffic and views from the road and made them regret agreeing to it or increased the likelihood they would make a complaint.

Some venues – shopping centres and events – have their own requirements around what the site needs to look like and bump in and out times that can greatly affect the time needed on the day. Sometimes, these locations like you to be there when the centre or event starts until the event or trade closes.

Who owns the location

You might be surprised who owns the specific location of your proposed pop up location. The following is a quick reference guide for who owns what and the likely cost and booking time required for the site.

Location and ownership	Cost range	Booking time	Set-up nuances
Shopping centres – privately owned. There can be some sections controlled by Council (pedestrian outstands, car parking)	Free–$500	Usually a month for smaller centres, where community use or kiosk hire is not common; role shared across multiple centres	Bump in before trade and leave after trade (sometimes). Strict visual requirements (sometimes). Strict approaching rules (sometimes).
Community market or festival – usually a community group if not Rotary Club	Free–$150	Booking process is always smooth; however, they confirm sites and vendors usually in the week prior	Preference to bump in before market or event starts and stay until the end. Usually won't know exact location until the days prior

Car park or walkway in shopping strip – usually Council-owned and managed	Free (if own project)	Allow two weeks. Usually booked through Council department – may be a local laws or economic development	Surrounding traders are not notified, so make a point of letting them know when setting up. Often a space won't be reserved, so get there early to block out a car park if required.
Parks, reserves and playgrounds – ownership varies. It could be co-managed by Council and Parks Victoria or a water authority	Free	Can be an extensive process, as it is not common practice. You may be referred to events department that manages weddings or photography.	Finding the right person in the organisation to speak to.

Criteria when considering locations:

- Weather. Even if there is shelter, people are unlikely to be in the park on a really hot or rainy day, so having a local backup can be good.
- Has the location been in the media recently? Is it prone to protestors, or has there been a recent decision that has created some community tension? (For example, safe injecting rooms)
- Is the location accessible in terms of physical and financial access? Some venues or events attract an entry fee for participants, which can mean you are restricting who can speak to you.
- Expected foot traffic at the specified pop up time. (Sometimes school holidays can be an advantage or disadvantage when it comes to foot traffic.)
- Choose times when passers-by can stop and chat (For example, after an event rather than when people rush to arrive and get inside, or at a train station in the evening, unless you're just handing out flyers in the morning).
- Seasonal weather conditions (for example: bush fires, extreme heat, snow, floods, storms, etc.). If necessary, consider an Emergency Management Plan.[3]
- Availability of toilets for staff and access to power, water, shade and public transport if required.

Everyone in your organisation will likely have a strong opinion on the location of your pop up; in client conversations, this can be one of the first areas of focus. In my experience, one of the common requests is having the pop up at the exact site of the

---

[3] business.gov.au, Develop an Emergency Management Plan, 2024, https://business.gov.au/planning/business-plans/develop-an-emergency-management-plan.

project. Sometimes this is great, particularly if it is generally a great location, but if it's a building site or no one is going to be there at the time of your pop up, then there is no point.

People have imagination, and with some graphics and a good map, they can put themselves into the space you are talking about without physically being there. Focus on the people, users or desired users you want to speak to and find a location to match.

Sometimes there is fear, perceived or real, about the location. Last time there might have been conflict, or you expect there to be conflict, because of a recent change of service or change in general. The mood in a community can change, and avoiding an area because of community outrage is not going to repair relationships or rebuild trust. Consider putting in place some of the learnings from Chapter 1: 'Keep yourself and others safe'. Focus on the people, users or desired users you want to speak to and if this is where you'll find them, then you gotta go!

Very rarely will you be the only project that needs to speak to your community or stakeholders. Sometimes project teams avoid an **excellent** location because another project team is already consulting on a project or there is a project happening or in the works (e.g. streetscape project). They don't want to create additional confusion and end up avoiding the location. Again, if the people you need or want to speak to are here, then you gotta go!

A couple of things that can help: Bring a member of the project team along to help with any specific questions about the project if there is a project being implemented in the area. That way, after participants have their questions answered, you can redirect their focus towards your project. If there is another consultation in the same space you can relocate; make sure you each know what the other is talking about and be prepared to talk to participants about both projects.

Sometimes the space set aside for your pop up just won't work at the location. Some organisations and teams find it difficult to staff pop ups outside of business hours when some locations only come alive at these times. If the location you need to visit at 10 am on a Wednesday is likely to be poorly attended, there are plenty of other locations that will be filled with people – coffee shops, shopping centres, community centres or libraries.

Take action

One of the best things we created within our organisation is a database of all the locations we have visited, nuances about the site, observations and recorded participants at the time of visiting. We keep this updated and, over the years, have built a library of intel we refer to when considering locations.

If you haven't got something like this in place already, do your future self and future colleagues a favour and create one. You can download the exact spreadsheet we use here: www.conversationco.com.au/slpop. Once developed, save it in your internal drive, then send the spreadsheet to everyone who has ever delivered a pop up or intercept in your organisation and ask them to fill it in. Keep it updated every time you do a pop up or intercept, and refer back to it when booking your next events.

In the next chapter, I talk about some of the interpersonal skills needed and how to assess your team's skill level.

Chapter 6

Not-so soft skills

Gone are the days when technical skills alone guaranteed success. Today, skills like empathy, adaptability and effective communication are just as vital for building trust and connection. In community engagement, these skills often get put to the test, and that's where the magic (or challenge) happens. It's interesting, isn't it, that these essential abilities are still referred to as *soft* skills? Personally, I think they should be called something like 'skills for survival' or 'the world's most essential skills'.

If you have a genuine interest in people and a knack for making others feel welcome, you're already halfway there. Engaging with someone one-on-one can be a great first step, especially if you're paired with someone experienced who can jump in if a topic gets heated. Practising these skills makes them second nature. So, if you bring a little extra emotional intelligence, empathy and communication into each interaction, your experiences – and theirs – will be far richer.

I think back to times when I've been called in after a team hit a nerve in the community – often unintentionally.

'People are really upset. How can we fix it?'

'Well, what happened?'

'We thought the community would love this idea, so we went ahead and closed access to their shops and homes for six weeks. We sent them a letter about the good news.'

Mastering these skills helps you create smoother, more meaningful interactions with the people you serve. Here's why honing these 'skills to thrive and survive' pays off:

- **Better communication:** Clarity, respect and connection foster understanding, reduce misunderstandings and build bridges.
- **Relatability:** Showing emotional intelligence, confidence and adaptability helps people see you as approachable.
- **Conflict resolution:** Learning how to listen, de-escalate and manage emotions improves customer service and leaves people feeling heard.
- **Critical thinking:** Being able to analyse and adapt in real time lets you tackle any curveball with confidence.

Now, let's dive into some real-world scenarios where we had to put these skills to the test at pop up events:

1. **Dogs joining the fun:** When participants bring their dogs, we sometimes have to ask them to keep their pets outside the pop up space. To keep everyone happy, we'll offer a solution like walking their dog or setting up a tie-off spot nearby.

Skills in action: problem-solving, adaptability, emotional intelligence

2. **Flat tyre rescue:** Once, a client had a flat tyre just as the pop up wrapped up. Two team members jumped in to fix it, which wasn't in the day's plan but was a great team moment.

   Skills in action: leadership, collaboration, problem-solving

3. **Emotional support needed:** A hairdresser shared that her business was struggling, which brought her to tears. We offered a private space to continue her story, giving her dignity and understanding.

   Skills in action: empathy, teamwork, adaptability

4. **Getting youth engaged:** At one pop up, we noticed we weren't reaching young people – a key target audience. We quickly adapted, grabbing some snacks and lollies to draw them in.

   Skills in action: adaptability, decision-making, responsiveness to social cues

5. **Improving accessibility on the fly:** A participant pointed out that the set-up wasn't friendly for older folks or easy for conversations. We adjusted, moving closer to public seating while keeping part of the team in the original location.

   Skills in action: creativity, resourcefulness, openness to feedback

Sound familiar? Maybe, but these little moments make a big difference. In this chapter, we'll break down what these skills are, why they're so critical to community engagement, and how to develop them within yourself and your team.

What are soft skills?

Let's redefine soft skills. Soft skills – well, let's call them the 'skills to thrive and survive' because that's exactly what they are – not just nice-to-haves. They're the very foundation of engaging, working with and understanding people. These aren't just traits you casually pick up; they're the human skills that make connection possible, and they're crucial in community engagement. Think of them as the tools that allow you to adapt, relate and respond in ways that make people feel valued.

Here are some core skills to thrive and survive that will make a difference in your community work.

1. Communication

Effective communication is the heart of every strong relationship. When you're out in the field, it's about so much more than delivering information. You need to understand the community's concerns, read their reactions and communicate in a way that's clear, empathetic and responsive.

Communication skills you'll use in the field:
- **Active listening:** Sometimes, people express their views through stories, anecdotes or concerns that might not seem directly related at first. Listening for the deeper message helps you understand their real perspective and shows respect for their lived experience.
- **Verbal communication:** Adjusting your style is essential. Some people want the short version, while others need a detailed breakdown. Your tone, pace and

word choice can make all the difference in connecting effectively.

- **Non-verbal communication:** Believe it or not, people pick up on your every move – crossed arms, facial expressions, even eye rolls (yes, they notice). I once saw someone get an earful after a participant caught them rolling their eyes. This is a reminder of how vital congruence is between our words and actions.
- **Written communication:** Writing for community engagement means thoughtfully capturing voices, stories and perspectives. Whether it's project materials or notes from conversations, clear and tailored writing makes a lasting impression.

2. Leadership

In community engagement, leadership isn't about having a title. It's about showing up, guiding others and creating a space where everyone can feel part of the conversation. Leadership is often about the little moments that keep the team motivated and on course – like cheering on a colleague who's had a tough day or coaching a team through a high-stakes engagement.

Key leadership skills you'll need in the field:
- **Problem-solving:** When things go wrong (and they will), taking the lead to find solutions shows commitment.
- **Coaching:** Helping team members grow is a core part of leadership. Sometimes, it's as simple as offering a listening ear or giving tips on handling tricky conversations.
- **People management:** Understanding each person's strengths and needs lets you support your team while achieving shared goals.

3. Teamwork

Community engagement is rarely a solo act. When you're in the field, good teamwork can make or break an event. Recognising when to step in – and when to step back – is crucial. Sometimes, a teammate might be more relatable to a particular participant, or you might need to switch roles to support a colleague who needs a moment to regroup.

Why teamwork matters in pop ups:
- **Conflict resolution:** Working closely in community settings means you'll sometimes need to help manage misunderstandings.
- **Mediation:** Keeping conversations smooth and positive among team members is crucial to creating a welcoming environment for participants.
- **Accountability:** Being reliable and consistent builds trust within the team, especially in high-stakes or stressful moments.

4. Creativity

Creativity isn't just for artists; it's a survival skill in community engagement! When you're faced with unexpected situations, thinking outside the box can lead to solutions you'd never considered. Sometimes, a little creativity is all it takes to turn a challenging interaction into a positive experience.

Must-have items in your pop up creativity toolkit:
- Cable ties of different lengths, because you never know what needs securing.

- Gaffer tape in black and a fun colour – perfect for quick fixes and a bit of flair.
- Lollies. These might seem trivial, but they're surprisingly effective icebreakers!
- Fold-up chairs. Two can be a game changer for creating a comfortable space.

5. Time management

When you're managing a pop up, time management isn't just about sticking to a schedule. It's about pacing your interactions so that everyone feels valued, and you're able to achieve your engagement goals without feeling rushed or stressed.

Allowing enough time to set up, engage and pack down makes for smoother operations. In my experience, when people see you're prepared and present, they feel more welcome and are more likely to open up. Avoiding the feeling of being rushed can make all the difference to both the team's and the public's experience.

6. Problem-solving

Problems will pop up – pun intended! Whether it's a location snafu, a tech glitch or a participant with unexpected needs, problem-solving skills let you keep things moving forward. Creative thinking and adaptability often go hand in hand here.

Here are example scenarios to problem-solve:
- The venue you planned to use suddenly becomes unavailable.

- A key piece of display equipment breaks just before the event.
- An interested group announces they're coming to protest, and you need to recalibrate quickly.

7. Work ethic

Pop ups can be hard work. You're on your feet, outdoors and sometimes dealing with a string of rejections. Having a strong work ethic keeps you motivated and positive, which has a noticeable impact on the people you engage with. When participants see your dedication, it reflects positively on the organisation you represent and builds credibility and trust.

How to demonstrate a strong work ethic:
- **Presentation:** Looking neat and professional shows respect for your role and the community.
- **Focus on comfort:** Helping participants settle in – whether that means moving a shopping trolley or getting children set up with an activity – creates a welcoming space.
- **Endurance:** Pop ups can be tough, especially when engagement is slow. Staying enthusiastic and willing to connect, even after some rejection, goes a long way.
- **Commitment:** Arriving early, staying late and keeping information accessible even while packing up are all part of a strong work ethic. You'd be surprised how many people come to chat just as you're about to leave!

8. Critical thinking

Critical thinking lets you respond strategically to feedback and adapt on the fly. This skill helps you connect the dots between what people are sharing and what the project needs, allowing you to gather meaningful input and insights that might otherwise be missed.

How critical thinking shapes community engagement:
- **Analysing responses:** When participants share stories or experiences, critical thinking helps you extract the underlying themes or issues that are relevant to the project.
- **Synthesising feedback:** Listening isn't just about taking notes; it's about understanding and summarising key points, then reflecting them back to confirm understanding.
- **Encouraging deeper reflection:** Sometimes, it's helpful to ask questions that prompt participants to think more deeply about their own viewpoints, which can lead to more valuable insights.

9. Conflict management

When dealing with the public, conflict can sometimes arise, especially in sensitive or highly impactful projects. Conflict management skills let you navigate these situations calmly, maintaining respect and understanding. Often, it's about finding common ground and seeing things from the participant's perspective.

Conflict management essentials in community engagement:
- **Empathy:** Understanding the participant's perspective can de-escalate tension and create a constructive environment.
- **Negotiation:** Sometimes, a compromise or a different approach can help satisfy both parties' needs.
- **Conflict resolution:** Staying calm, patient and open to solutions help manage disagreements effectively.

10. Emotional Intelligence

Emotional intelligence (EI) is the ability to recognise, understand and manage both your own emotions and others'. It's an especially valuable skill when you're working with diverse groups or sensitive topics. In community engagement, EI helps you gauge how participants feel and thoughtfully respond. It's about being in tune with the social dynamics at play and adjusting your approach to ensure positive, productive interactions.

Core components of emotional intelligence in community engagement:
- **Self-awareness:** Being mindful of your own emotional triggers and biases helps you respond rather than react in challenging situations. It's a reminder that even on a tough day, our tone, body language and words can impact the people we engage with.
- **Empathy:** Showing empathy means acknowledging the feelings and perspectives of others, making participants feel valued and heard.
- **Social skills:** Building rapport and creating connections can make a big difference in how receptive participants are to sharing their honest views.

Together, these components build a foundation for respectful, effective interactions that can make even difficult conversations constructive. Emotional intelligence underpins every soft skill and plays a huge role in creating trust and rapport in the field.

Bridging skills to thrive and survive with real-world engagement

Now that we've explored these soft skills, let's see how they translate into tangible outcomes for community engagement. In practical terms, each skill contributes to creating an experience where participants feel respected, informed and encouraged to contribute.

Better connection with participants

Having a team with strong interpersonal skills means that each person brings warmth, patience and adaptability to their interactions. This isn't just about being pleasant, it's about creating a space where people feel truly heard. When participants sense that we're genuinely interested in their thoughts and feelings, they're more likely to share openly, which leads to richer insights and better outcomes.

Enhancing team dynamics

A well-rounded team leverages each member's strengths. With soft skills in the mix, there's an ease to collaboration that makes each engagement feel cohesive. A team that values communication, respect and accountability makes participants feel more comfortable and supported, as well as strengthens each other in their roles.

Building Community Trust

When we apply these skills thoughtfully, we don't just gather feedback; we build trust. Every interaction in a pop up is a reflection of the organisation we represent, and these seemingly small moments can make a significant difference to the community's perception. When participants see our dedication, empathy and professionalism, it can foster a sense of trust that goes beyond individual projects.

Taking soft skills beyond the pop up

While we've focused on soft skills in the context of pop ups, these skills are valuable in every aspect of community engagement – and life. They help us navigate not only our professional lives but also our personal relationships, encouraging us to approach each interaction with empathy, understanding and adaptability.

Whether you're just starting out or looking to deepen your expertise, honing these skills will create lasting, positive impacts. You'll build a reputation as someone who truly values the voices of others, someone who can handle the unexpected and someone who understands that great engagement is more than a job; it's a commitment to making meaningful connections.

Rate your own skills

This quiz is a reflection tool, helping you consider both your own behaviours and those within your team when engaging the community in listening posts, pop ups or intercepts.

For each question, rate yourself based on how often the described behaviour happens. Score yourself as follows:
- 1 point: Rarely/No
- 2 points: Sometimes/Occasionally
- 3 points: Often/Most of the time
- 4 points: Always

At the end, total your points to get feedback on your skill levels.

Communication
1. When listening to community members, do you listen to understand their perspectives rather than just appeasing them or quickly providing information?
2. Do you find that community members generally understand the project and the information you want or need from them?
3. Is the feedback you receive on-topic and directly relevant to the project?

Total for Communication: _____

Leadership
1. Do you typically take the lead in decision-making, even if it's not your project?
2. Does your team regularly look to you for guidance or direction?
3. Do you and your team members take turns briefing new members or offering feedback on each other's conversations?

Total for Leadership: _____

Teamwork
1. Do all team members equally take ownership of the project when out in the community?
2. Is there a shared commitment among team members to reach desired engagement outcomes or capture diverse community views?

Total for Teamwork: _____

Creativity
1. When faced with unusual requests or situations, does your team tend to consider alternative solutions rather than dismissing them?

Total for Creativity: _____

Time Management
1. Do you and your team members consistently arrive on time?
2. Do you find that participants always have sufficient time to participate after you've explained the activity?

Total for Time Management: _____

Problem-Solving
- Rate your team's likelihood of solving these issues.
  - The site is closed or cannot be accessed.
  - A key piece of equipment breaks, altering the way you display materials.
  - The owner of the site has no idea you're coming and refuses you entry.

- The location has been boycotted by an interested group.

Total for Problem-Solving: _____

Work Ethic
1. Do you/your team consistently show these behaviours? (Add points for each 'always')
   - Dress and appear professional.
   - Avoid eating or drinking during the pop up.
   - Go out of the way to ensure participants are comfortable.
   - Engage actively, even after rejections.
   - Arrive early and leave late.
   - Remain open to interaction while packing up.

Total for Work Ethic: _____

Critical Thinking
1. Do you/your team easily connect community feedback with relevant project aspects?
2. Do you/your team effectively relate what community members are saying to the project?
3. Are you/they able to summarise participants' points clearly and accurately?

Total for Critical Thinking: _____

Conflict Management
1. I continue the conversation or seek support from a colleague if a participant becomes vocal or physical in their body movements.

   2.   When I face conflict I remain calm and unchanged on the surface.

Total for Conflict Management: _____

Emotional Intelligence

   1.   How often do you reflect on how your behaviour impacts those around you?

   2.   If something doesn't go to plan, do you work through scenarios or try to identify external sources of blame?

   3.   Do you find it easy to find something in common with a stranger?

Total for Emotional Intelligence: _____

Scoring and Reflection

Add up your points from each section for a final score. Then, reflect on your results using the scale below.

- 40–60 points: Strong foundation! You're building a solid set of soft skills. Reflect on any areas with lower scores to focus on growth opportunities.
- 61–80 points: Great work! You're showing strong capabilities across most areas. Keep practising to finetune your skills.
- 81–100 points: Excellent! You have a well-rounded skill set that likely makes a positive impact in every interaction. Keep honing these abilities for continued success in community engagement.

Develop your team's soft skills

Improving soft skills starts with a commitment to self-reflection and a willingness to grow. Whether you're leading a team or are part of one, there are plenty of ways to encourage growth in these essential skills. Here are a few approaches that can help build a culture of skill development and continuous improvement.

1. Embrace feedback

Feedback can come from a colleague, supervisor or even indirectly through a community member's response. Being open to it helps you adapt and refine your approach. Next time you're out at a pop up, try asking a colleague for specific feedback – like how well you communicated, approached leadership or applied critical thinking.

Another way is to set aside time for team reflection after each pop up. A post-event debrief is a great way to structure this process. Debriefs give everyone a chance to reflect on their soft skills and share constructive feedback with each other. Encourage team members to share their observations on what went well, what challenges arose and how it could be improved, how they handled different interactions, and any observations on communication, teamwork or conflict management.

Reflection not only helps team members process their experiences but also builds a culture of openness and improvement.

2. Communicate regularly and purposefully

Even when you're handling individual tasks, use opportunities to connect with your team. Practise communicating in different formats – whether face-to-face, via email or presenting to a group.

Each form of communication has its nuances, so trying a variety helps you become more versatile and effective.

As you communicate, be mindful of your tone, clarity and the way you're addressing others. Notice what works well for others, too, and experiment with their tips or techniques to develop a style that suits you.

3. Build positive relationships

Strong relationships are the backbone of most soft skills. Building rapport with colleagues, team members and managers makes collaborative work smoother and more enjoyable. Start by having genuine conversations – ask about their weekend, family or hobbies. To expand these connections, consider joining a group activity or volunteering, which can introduce you to a broader range of interactions and topics.

Relationships strengthen with small, consistent interactions, so even casual chats can add up to more meaningful connections over time.

4. Step out of your comfort zone

To improve, sometimes you need to challenge yourself with something unfamiliar. If decision-making isn't your strong suit, try taking the lead on a small task or decision. Or, if you're used to being the decision-maker, let others take the reins while you observe and support.

Growth often happens when we step into roles that push us. It's in these moments that we learn the most about our own strengths, areas for improvement and the potential we hadn't yet tapped.

5. Learn by observing others

Look around for someone who demonstrates the soft skills you admire, and observe their approach. Watch how they engage a community member, manage a tough conversation or explain something complex in a simple way.

By observing, you can pick up nuances that aren't always obvious. Jot down what you notice – maybe it's their tone, patience or the questions they ask. Later, try incorporating one or two of these behaviours into your own approach and see what resonates.

6. Adjust your self-talk

Our inner dialogue can be one of our biggest hurdles. If you tend to be hard on yourself, try adding the word *yet* to your self-criticism: 'I'm not great at managing conflict yet.' Or, imagine how you'd speak to a friend in the same situation – kindly, with encouragement.

Shifting your self-talk is a small but powerful change that helps build confidence. It reminds you that skill-building is a journey; and progress, however small, is still progress.

7. Role-play scenarios

One of the best ways to prepare for real-world engagement is through role-playing. Set up scenarios where team members can practise handling common pop up situations, from managing conflict to engaging a disengaged audience. This kind of practice allows people to try out different responses in a safe environment and can lead to insightful discussions about what worked and what didn't.

8. Offer personalised skill development

People bring different strengths to the table, and individualised training can enhance these. Some might benefit from practising communication strategies, while others could work on adaptability or conflict resolution. Tailoring development opportunities to the needs of each person creates a well-rounded, resilient team.

Take action

Try a quick self-reflection and choose one thing you'd like to do differently at your next community engagement. In the next chapter, we'll look at the different types of people you need on your team for pop ups, so think about the skills we've covered here and how to bring a good mix to your team.

Mother and child learning more about a smoke free city

April's first job

Caravan before being reskinned

**Celebrating with the neighbours after
8 months of construction noise**

Who doesn't love a mascot!

**Drew getting crafty
with bending timber**

Drews handy work and seat design

Elaine using her head during the rennovation

Helping keep Drew calm

Hours of nailing

I bought a template

Complex installation and bump in, in the middle of the City

**Return to face-to-face post Covid19
lockdowns and wearing masks**

Intense rust removal

**My wonderful mum making buttons,
to meet our hard deadline**

Crafty engagement during Covid-19 surfboard prop for the win (not staged!)

Uncle Fred made 'millimetre' perfect windows with a difficult brief

We bought a template

Chapter 7

Work to your team's strengths

Imagine going to work each day and not knowing what is expected of you, how to prepare yourself or what success looks like. Think about the topics that generate the most consultation work and their primary skills – engineers, transport planners, urban designers, asset owners. Sure, some of these fields cross over into the humanities, but for many, working this closely with the public will be uncomfortable. We need to spend time making sure teams are adequately prepared for their role and what is expected of them.

I would much rather someone tell me where their skills and expertise lie so that I can identify how to best use them at a pop up and how to best support them. Identifying the roles you need at your pop up and who you need in each of those roles will contribute to the success of your engagement program. Getting this right is key to people sticking their hand up again and making themselves available for a pop up.

Knowing the skills and expertise you need on your pop up team will:

- allow you to plan ahead of time for the roles you need and the staffing mix you need to fill the pop up
- increase the comfort and future willingness of people to volunteer in participating at pop ups
- give your community stakeholders a better experience at your pop up because they will be able to have their needs met
- make sure staff are not outnumbering the number of participants or crowding out the physical space.

We also need a combination of personality types and expertise, as the people we are speaking with are all going to need something different from us (see Chapter 10).

Our brains are hardwired for efficiency. One of the ways it does this is by grouping new experiences into experiences we've had before. Our brains also do this with people. We seek out people similar to ourselves and perceive them to be less of a threat.

I regularly see and experience this at pop ups – someone quieter or more detail-oriented will gravitate to the same kind of person at a pop up, and vice versa. If I corner that kind of person, I will struggle to get more than 10 words from them, but as soon as they are with a person they connect with, the conversation will flow.

Our organisation knows the effectiveness of this, so much so that we've employed specific conversation facilitators for the project – a young person to be more relatable, local people from the area or someone with a similar cultural background – even if there are no language barriers.

In this chapter we will work through the:
- core roles within your pop up
- responsibilities of each role
- desired personality traits of individuals to fill the role
- ways to upskill and brief staff.

Core roles within your pop up

The roles you need will depend on:
- **the complexity of the project:** Is it easy enough for anyone to explain, or do you need a core member of the project team or someone else with specialist skills in the topic?
- **what else is happening in that area:** Are there other projects that the community are likely to have questions about?
- **the stage of the project:** Often, the further along in the project's phase, the more nuanced the information needed and the more detailed feedback can be. For example, at the start, you might be more interested in a person's experiences and what they believe might be needed to solve a particular challenge. As the project progresses, you might return with options that require a more detailed understanding of them.

If any of the above situations are true for your project, consider increasing the technical expertise within. Even if these individuals are not as comfortable holding a conversation, the people you are speaking with will appreciate having the technical answers to their questions.

Generally, the roles we suggest having at a pop up include:

The technical expert

This person is usually a core part of the project team. Nobody knows the project better than them. Perhaps they've written the report or have the technical know-how and are able to answer all the in-depth questions the public may have about the project. We typically partner them with a people expert, who can help bring their nuanced understanding of people to the conversation and ensure feedback is collected consistently and any conflict is managed.

Favourable personality traits:
- Well-developed communication skills (able to present complex topics, clearly and simply).
- Experience in your topic of expertise.
- Patient and able to explain complex topics to general community members with little or no experience.

Responsibilities of this role:
Initially, you might want to pair up with the people expert if you feel less confident about speaking with the public. If you are feeling confident, start approaching people and encouraging them to ask questions or provide their feedback.

Do's for the technical expert:
- Keep deferring to the community's opinions. Once they know you are an expert, they are bound to keep asking for your opinion. Unless the purpose is to strengthen understanding, keep directing the conversation back to their opinion.
- Don't get defensive. It's hard when you have put your heart and soul into the project, and within the first five

minutes you hear a complaint. Use this as an opportunity to get some direct feedback – 'What could we change so it got your support?', 'What would help you understand this better?'.
- Take this opportunity to listen directly to the community and their needs or concerns.

The people expert
This person is usually responsible for supporting delivery of the organisation's community engagement projects. This person usually has well-developed soft skills (Chapter 6) and uses their emotional intelligence to manage tricky conversations and help the technical expert to provide the right level of information – not so detailed as to have lost interest, not too brief or surface-level to create concern.

Favourable personality traits:
- Well-developed people skills (interpersonal, communication skills).
- Confident in approaching people on the street.
- Able to build rapport easily.
- Patient and able to provide clear instruction to others on the day.

Responsibilities of this role:
Initially, you might want to pair up with the technical expert. You can get across the details of the project and check in on the level of comfort your technical expert has with holding conversations.

Once everything is moving well, you might like to channel a nightclub promoter and work to bring more people into the pop up itself. Or, if the location you are in is a bit quieter, you could take some engagement materials to nearby shopfronts to engage more people.

Do's for the people expert:
Don't run yourself into the ground; make sure you have a break.

- Pick the conversations you want to have. If you know there is a passionate community member whom you have spoken to multiple times and need a break, that's okay.
- Move around the engagement activities. Don't feel you need to stay at the trickiest station.
- Use quiet moments to debrief with technical experts about where you might have intervened or something you noticed – eye roll, a defensive reaction.
- Take your own notes of improvements, but avoid getting too detailed during the pop up. Remember, you are there to support the team and no one wants to feel they are being watched!

Connected projects or expertise (AKA the third wheel)
The third wheel is there just in case the project or the skills they have come up in conversation. People won't know how valuable the third wheel's presence is because, to them, it will seem like this person gave a few quick answers and people were on their way.

When this person is not there and there is another big project happening nearby, or soon to be happening, people are not able to move on to participate, as they become absorbed in needing their questions answered. Without the third wheel, colleagues will be left scrolling through the company website trying to get an update, leaving the participant questioning how others in the organisation don't know x, y, z about the topic. Trust us, we are glad third wheels are there.

Favourable personality traits:
- Well-developed communication skills (able to present complex topics, clearly and simply).
- Experience in your topic of expertise.
- Patient and able to explain complex topics to general community members with little or no experience.

Responsibilities of this role:
Shadow the technical expert or the people expert. Once you feel like you have the hang of the project, feel free to go solo. Keep a lookout for anyone who might need your help with a technical question. If you do, try to excuse yourself from the conversation you are having or wait for the appropriate time.

Do's for the third wheel:
- Don't be weird and hang off to the side. It will make you look like a security guard. Also, people will question your work ethic.
- Read up about the project and be prepared to pitch in and help people participate in the activities.
- Don't insert information about your project (unprompted), unless it is related or the community has questions. Let's use the time to focus on the project we are there to engage on.
- Take your own notes, particularly where feedback might have a crossover into your project – perhaps you are hearing ways the community likes to be kept updated or the material or colour preferences that might inform what you do.

The extra hand or the ring in

The extra hand is the one who hasn't expected to receive a text message asking them to come along to a pop up. Jenny was sick, Fred had a soccer game with his son, and they're the only hope. Breathe. It's going to be okay. There are some advantages to their involvement; they won't be too close to the project yet will get the hang of it and its activities pretty fast.

Favourable personality traits:
- Studied improvisation or theatre (just kidding).
- Openness to learning.
- Well-developed people skills (interpersonal, communication skills).
- Confident in approaching people on the street.

Responsibilities of this role:
Shadow the technical expert or the people expert. Once you feel like you have the hang of the project, feel free to go solo. You want to position yourself at a station if the pop up is set up in that manner. For example, at the entry, so you can welcome people into the space and explain how to participate.

Do's for the extra hand or ring in:
- Shadow either the people expert or the technical expert, depending on which skills you want to develop.
- Start by taking notes and listening to what the community is saying. Read back what you have written to ensure it captures their viewpoint.
- Smile and be warm in your invitation. We always need someone on the outside of the pop up, inviting people in. Imagine you are a concierge at a ritzy hotel.

- Ask for help if you find yourself with a passionate community member or with a question you cannot answer. Excuse yourself and ask someone in the team for help, stay and listen, then you will know the answer next time.
- Relax, and the conversations will flow easier. The more relaxed you feel, the more comfortable people will be engaging with you.

The political minder

Depending on how busy the pop up is likely to be (chances are it's busy if you are inviting a politician, photographer or council official), you may or may not need this extra role. However, it can be useful to have someone dedicated to supporting this person at a pop up. They may want to take photos with participants at the event, listen in on what people are saying or speak to a different audience (perhaps going in and out of shops).

Favourable personality traits:
- Comfortable with executives or senior leaders.
- Well-developed people skills (interpersonal, communication skills).
- Confident in approaching people on the street.

Responsibilities of this role:
This role is about ensuring that your VIP gets what they need from the experience or what participants expect from them. It will depend on who your VIP is – if it's the media or a photographer, they will want photos and footage from the day, so you will likely have to ask people's permission to take their photo or capture them having a conversation. You might need to then collect necessary paperwork – photo permission forms, etc.

If your VIP is a politician or executive, they will likely want to listen in on some conversation but not directly be the person answering all the questions, so you'll want to bring them into a conversation someone else is having through a quick introduction and a question like 'Do you mind if we listen in?'. Depending on the length of time they are staying at the pop up, you may shadow them the whole time, noting down feedback someone provides while they have the conversation.

Do's for the minder:
- Make sure you are well-versed with the project, do the same reading and attend the same briefings as the other team members. You may need to answer even more technical questions or hold your own conversations.
- Arrive early before your VIP, and shadow the technical expert to understand any detail around the activities.
- When your VIP arrives, introduce yourself and find out some more details about their visit purpose (how long they have to spend onsite, what they would like to get out of their visit).
- Introduce your VIP to the rest of the project team and give them a rundown of the engagement activities and the project (it's safe to assume they have some knowledge through a briefing paper, however, will likely not have the detail).

Ways to upskill and brief staff

Have some basic training in approaching people or some exposure. Some sites – shopping centres or main street environments – can be the toughest locations to engage. Often, our clients can't believe the level of rejection faced within a shopping centre environment.

For all staff, we provide a briefing document that covers the details of the project (project scope, what can and cannot be influenced by the consultation), the activities and the site-specific information (car parking, availability of toilets, etc), and the process for following up enquiries (sometimes an online form or paper form).

Once onsite, do a briefing and run through the activities, as they are set up in any order, encourage people to work in pairs initially, and shadow one another while working and having solo conversations.

There are a few areas you need all staff to be versed in:
- Who your onsite experts are. How can they get support with a technical or non-project-related question?
- Process for managing conflict (your protocol from Chapter 1: 'Keep yourself and others safe').
- Ways to keep the dialogue going once the get-to-know-you chatter ends and how to best introduce the project questions.
- Protocols to keep themselves and others safe:
  - Pre-pop up checklist.
  - Incident/Injury Form
  - Child Safety Reporting Procedure/Policy
  - Near Miss Form

Here are some questions you might have about setting your team up for success:

My project has nothing to do with children. Is child safety still important?

Please defer to your organisational policy or procedure on child safety; however, when in the community, we have an obligation to report perceived or observed incidents of child abuse, whether they occur at the engagement activity or are disclosed to us during discussions with a child or young person. When you're working in the community it's important to recognise the potential signs of child abuse. Here are some examples of behaviour that *may* indicate child abuse:

- showing wariness and distrust of adults
- demanding or aggressive behaviour
- low self-esteem
- difficulty relating to adults and peers
- having broken bones or unexplained bruising, burns or welts in different stages of healing
- being unable to explain an injury, or providing explanations that are inconsistent, vague or unbelievable
- being withdrawn or overly obedient
- being reluctant to go home
- creating stories, poems or artwork about abuse
- perpetrating abuse on other young people (may be repeating behaviour they have experienced)

For more information about the signs of child abuse visit https://www.vic.gov.au/child-protection-early-childhood-protect/identify-signs-child-abuse

I don't have all those people available.

Having two people, let alone four or five people, can be a bit of a stretch at a pop up. Sometimes, at locations that are small or likely to have less people, having four or five people is not appropriate anyway.

Think about the people you absolutely need there. It's usually a technical expert and a people expert. If reaching more people is a key measure, consider how you can extend your reach on the day. Can you make the activity self-sufficient? Can you have materials that people can take with them if the two of you are deep in conversation and unable to help a third person?

There'll be more staff than people if I bring that entourage along.

You might want to reread Chapter 5: 'Selecting the right location' and make sure the location is the right fit for your project. Quieter locations are great if you want to have detailed conversations or if you are actively bringing in a different community group into the project.

As above, think about how to make the activities self-sufficient or obvious for people to participate in without your direct involvement. Or perhaps you can use excess people to go and speak to nearby business owners. Reflect on the role you typically play when working at pop ups, roles you wished you had onsite, or people you imagine would be a good fit for those roles. Other skill sets you might like to include may be speaking a common language in the community you are working with.

In the next chapter, I talk more about human behaviour that will not only help you to engage participants but also your engagement team.

Chapter 8

Engage human nature

It's well accepted that the marketing industry uses behavioural theory to track our desires, urges and other subconscious factors. Then they use this information to influence our decisions, make us question our choices and leave us wondering why we have a trolley full of items when we just went to the store for one thing! Meanwhile, we, wholesome practitioners, submit our surveys for ethics approval, display and stick to what we say in our privacy policies and randomise questions to reduce any possibility of influencing someone's decision. Imagine if we kept our strong ethical hearts and filled our brains with what a consumer marketer knows. We'd be a force for good while not increasing consumer debt.

It's time to admit something. I quit community engagement back in 2017. You see, April the Caravan was going to be a cocktail van for a business I had registered called the Laughing Peacock! It was part of my escape plan. I wanted a change of scenery, as it felt like no matter what I did, the amount of pre-work with projects and carefully crafted key messages, the community was still angry, annoyed and frustrated. More projects were ending up in the media, coming across the desks of senior leaders or councillors, and this made it even tougher to convince project managers to get out in front of the community. Who could blame them? I almost felt relieved when, at the time, the only method they wanted was a survey!

My plan was to be Lady Peacock by night and on the weekends, and by day a Life Coach – I still liked people and wanted to work with them to create a bit of joy while doing something meaningful! I started studying human behaviour, and as I completed my practical assessments and classes, I could feel my sparkle returning. Still working in community engagement, I implemented what I was learning.

There is this one technique that is incredibly simple; it's called mirroring. Rather than using reasoning or throwing more information at the person, you repeat back in your own words what they tell you. No clever interpretations, no strategies for overcoming the problem – just listening and repeating.

As an example:

> Participant: 'I feel annoyed by all the development in my area.' You: 'You feel annoyed by the growth and development occurring in your area.' (you can ad lib a little and need a tone of empathy in your voice).

Mirroring is a connection builder because it lets people feel heard and understood, sometimes for the first time in their lives.

As community engagement practitioners, we are highly ethical people and make sure we are being clear and transparent with the information and what the community can and cannot influence. We will build trust, but without the foundation of connection, we are unlikely to establish this.

What probably makes mirroring so effective is just how bad most of us are at taking the time to really hear what those around us have to say. If you eavesdrop on any conversation, you can hear that people's responses are usually designed to put the spotlight back onto themselves.

This was one of many techniques or approaches that have great a crossover into our field – some I will share within this chapter.

> *'Unless someone like you cares an awful lot, nothing is going to get better. It's not.' – Dr Seuss*

While my newfound superpowers were not enough to keep me in my then-position as Internal Community Engagement Advisor, the new learnings were enough to keep me interested in the profession and boosted my engagement bag of tricks. I trust that integrating some of these ideas and techniques into your practice will:
- make it easier for the people you are engaging with to participate
- make you recognise your intrinsic needs and behaviours to be a better engagement practitioner
- create a better relationship with those around you – community, loved ones, friends
- increase participation in your engagement.

Consumer marketers study cognitive behaviour to determine our patterns and behaviours to increase sales, increase the speed of our decision-making and reduce regret (among lots of other things). Just for fun, after you finish reading – and only after you finish reading this chapter – look up *Understanding the Consumer Decision Making Process* and *buyer's remorse or cognitive dissonance*.

For our work in community engagement, particularly when we are working in small groups or one-to-one in a pop up environment, we have a greater ability to alter our approach to suit those we are with. This understanding will help you with all of your other engagement activities – surveying, large workshops or public meetings.

In this chapter you will learn to:
- identify and leverage the motivations of the person participating in your consultation
- connect to people by identifying which representational system they primarily use and then matching it.

I am going to get a bit woo-woo on you, so check your biases here.

Why are people really engaging?

The Six Core Needs is a concept first birthed by Sigmund Freud and modernised by Tony Robbins (keep reading; I promise this is some of his better work). The concept puts forward that people seek experiences to fulfil their need for connection, variety, significance, certainty, growth and contribution. The first four needs are essential, whereas growth and contribution are more altruistic – used by coaches to increase fulfilment (you can use these, though; keep reading). People will seek experiences that fulfil their need for the first four, whether in a constructive or harmful manner. The level sought will depend on what they are primarily driven by.

How does this relate to community engagement? Participating in a community engagement is a way for people to fulfil their needs. Similarly, their participation can be constructive or less constructive. Understanding a person's motivation can help you pitch your engagement project and connect the project back to something that matters.

Following are some dramatised response examples to a fictional question: 'What does your town need?'

'I've lived in this town for 70 years. My parents moved into this area when they first married. My grandparents are buried in the local cemetery. I have seen it all. Before Jeff Kennet amalgamated the councils, we were under the Shire of XYZ. I used to work in the roads department…'

If someone responds this way to my project question – answering the question without answering the question – I know they are using this community engagement activity to primarily meet their need for significance, secondary to their need for connection.

The next bit might seem a bit ingenuous to some; I would say something like 'Tell me, then – from all this experience (recognising their need for significance) …' then ask the question again. If there is still a lack of response, I might lean on their need for contribution and say, 'What is it you would like young people, or your grandchildren (if I have found that out already), to experience, then?'.

Here is a rundown of the four core needs:

Need for connection
Everyone needs to feel a connection with someone or something. The means for satisfying these needs can be good for us, those around us and society; they can also be neutral or negative for all.

Let's look at a few ways we can satisfy our need for connection by positive means:
- connection from immediate family members and/or close friends through quality time
- connection with community and/or work
- performing good deeds, like volunteering
- being kind or receiving kindness
- loving our pets
- connection to religion
- giving or receiving gifts.

By negative means, we can also achieve our need for connection by:
- dominating and controlling others
- being helpless, so people have to take care of us
- always talking about our illness (creates connection, love and empathy from others).

In a community engagement context, when I hear people say (in their opening sentence) 'My friend told me to sign up', 'I'm not sure what this is about. I came here with my neighbour', 'This property used to belong to the Barnes family', I will use this connection lens to support their participation. I might respond with 'Can you see your friend yet? Otherwise, I can take you through what we are doing.'

Need for variety
We all want and need variety in our lives, as it exercises our emotional, psychological, mental and physical range. The level we each require is different; for one person it could be the act of trying a different cafe, for another it could be participating in an extreme sport.

Let's look at a few ways we can satisfy our need for variety in a positive manner:
- different forms of exercise
- participating in a club
- attending live arts
- travelling
- learning a new hobby or skill
- watching the news, a quality TV show or movie

By negative means, we can also achieve our need for variety by:
- creating drama, conflict or problems
- emotional eating
- becoming overly excited during a crisis.

In a community engagement context, when I hear people say (in their opening sentence) 'This looks interesting. What's this all about?' or 'What bad decisions are you making now?', I will use this lens of variety to support their participation: 'Okay, well, let me take you through everything we are doing (or have available for you to participate).' (I wouldn't do this with our certainty friends, as it might initially be too overwhelming. See page 133).

Significance
Who doesn't like to feel special, significant or important to another person or group of people? To want to feel important doesn't make

you prideful, needy or a narcissist. We need to feel important, needed and wanted in life.

This need begins when we are infants; babies and children need to feel #1 in their caregivers' lives. It is part of our survival mechanism – to gain the attention of our caregivers so we get food, warmth and comfort through this attention. Lack of feeling significant is a form of low self-esteem because it stems from comparing ourselves to others. We begin to question our superiority, inferiority and, in the end, significance/importance.

On a positive note, this one element in life makes us raise our standards. On the flip side, if we become hyper-focused on significance, we develop difficulty connecting with others because comparisons breed differences, not commonalities.

Let's look at a few ways we can satisfy our need for significance in a positive manner:
- seeking meaning and purpose in work or volunteering opportunities (matters to us or others, the cause, people we work with)
- seeking to contribute to humanity (invention, research, breakthrough)
- being the best at something (athlete, business, work or personal life)

By negative means, we can also achieve our need for significance by:
- failure (some people feel significant if they are the worst at something. This brings them attention and help, which fosters feelings of significance)
- being the sickest in the group (for the same reason as above)

- by tearing down someone or something, trash talking about others' achievements or story topping to redirect the attention back to us and away from the other person's achievements.

In a community engagement context, when I hear people say (in their opening sentence) 'I helped to build this facility', 'Why wasn't I made aware of this?', 'I have lived in this area for 50 years. I have seen ...' or 'You will be hearing from my lawyers', I will use this lens of significance to support their participation by saying 'Sounds like we will really benefit from hearing about your experiences' or 'So sorry; glad you are here now as it seems as if you will have a lot to add.'

Certainty

Certainty is the desire to feel safe, to be comfortable in our environment and to experience pleasure while avoiding pain. With certainty, we feel stable, grounded, protected and secure, and we can predict certain necessary safeguards in our lives.

Like every other basic human need, the amount of certainty needed varies from person to person and is fulfilled in different ways. The human brain is not designed to handle great levels of uncertainty. There are many decisions out of our control, and there are often many variables for our decisions. Our quality of life depends on how well we adapt to uncertainty. If you handle uncertainty well, you will handle life well.

Let's look at a few ways we can satisfy our need for certainty in a positive manner:
- Having a budget so we can plan for the costs of life.
- Structuring our week and building in regular time for self-care.

- Maintaining close relationships with our family and friends.

By negative means, we can also achieve our need for certainty by:
- trying to control others (for example, trying to control a spouse out of fear of abandonment, failure, and such so you feel safe or have certainty)
- micromanaging (brings certainty that things will be done our way)
- withdrawing (brings certainty that we can control our life experiences by minimising our personal interactions).

In a community engagement context, when I hear people say (in their opening sentence) 'I have been so worried about this, I haven't been able to sleep', 'I've put my plans on hold until I could find out what this was about' or 'You will be hearing from my lawyers', I use this lens of certainty to support their participation and also to reassure them. 'Outcomes from this process will be used to x, y, z.' I would also try to find out what they are specifically concerned about and the level of direct impact on them.

You might like to reflect on what motivates you. Having a working understanding of this through your own self-reflection will make it easier for you to identify the needs of others. Use the above-mentioned core needs to connect with participants and keep them engaged in the project or engagement activity.

The two remaining needs are more altruistic; they are not as essential to everyone.
- **Growth:** Whatever you value in life – health, relationships, career success, integrity, contribution – must be cultivated, worked, practised or expanded. In community

engagement, we can remind participants of who they are becoming and the importance of contributing now.

- **Contribution:** Going beyond one's own needs and giving to others with no hope for or expected personal gain. It's contributing to other people, a cause or a movement.

When I hear people say (close-ish to their opening sentence) 'In 10 years' time I am likely to be dead', 'I have no idea what is needed', 'I've just moved to the area' or 'I have never done this before', I try to trigger the sense of growth or contribution to support their participation. 'You may be dead, but your children and grandchildren won't be. What do they need for their future?' If in a longer-term process, like sitting on a community panel, I would say, 'This will be new for a lot of people. You only need to be an expert in your own life and needs of your community.'

Help people understand better

We have to understand and be aware that everyone thinks and processes information differently. One of the many ways we are different is the way we learn, absorb and process information. Fleming and Mills (1992) explored how individuals understand themselves and the people around them through four different learning modes – **visual**, **auditory**, **kinesthetic** and **auditory digital**.

Knowing this helps you understand your preferred mode, which you will use predominantly in your interactions with others, and recognise your audience's preferred learning mode, which will guide you on how to best communicate with them.

As a community engagement practitioner, it is your responsibility to support participants to understand what you are consulting on and to support them to participate in a meaningful way. You can recognise a person's preferred learning/processing method by noticing patterns of eye movements and language speech patterns.

What are these styles?

Visual learners learn and process information by seeing visuals (maps, diagrams, images) and are less distracted by noise. They may have trouble remembering long verbal instructions, as their minds work harder to convert words into images.

A visual learner will look up to the sky when they are thinking or recalling memories. They will also use visual words in their speech, like *see, looks, appear, view, show me, dawn, reveal, imagine, illuminate, crystal clear.*

Auditory learners learn and process information verbally (listening to someone talk, listening to an audio recording) or through reading information. The auditory person can be distracted by noises and tone of voice. Words used are important, and they can easily pick up subtleties of language and inflection.

An auditory learner will look either left or right, towards their ears, when thinking or recalling information. Phrases you might hear in their speech are *that sounds good, I am all ears, that rings a bell.*

Kinesthetic learners learn and process information by practising or through physical movement. They do not typically respond well to pictures or verbal instructions and much prefer to learn by doing or moving while listening to information. A kinesthetic learner will look towards their navel when thinking or recalling information. They are much more likely to use words like *feel*, *grasp*, *get a hold of*, *catch on*, *tap into*, *concrete* or *solid* when confirming their understanding.

Auditory Digital learners are not as easy to pick, as they show signs from all other systems. They can work with a higher volume of information and data, and they memorise by creating or learning steps, systems and procedures for tasks. An auditory digital learner may struggle to interact socially and come across as dogmatic. As they are logic driven, they may become impatient with or find it hard to understand those who aren't.

In a community engagement context, you can support the varied learning styles by providing visual learners with maps, diagrams, videos or imagery, and auditory learners with the opportunity to listen to someone speak, a reading material or the opportunity to have a conversation one-on-one.

Supporting kinesthetic learners to engage in projects can be difficult. If the project relates to a physical location, you could consider a walking tour where you physically move around the site and the project can be experienced firsthand. Otherwise, following the advice in Chapter 9: 'Rooms within rooms', you can create a trail within your pop up, requiring movement between stations. To support auditory digital learners, it is about recognising and providing the level of detail required to understand the project and what is being asked of them.

Giving people the nudge

Nudge Theory describes the way a small change can alter people's behaviour in a predictable way without taking away their choice. It has been widely used in consumer marketing, particularly within supermarkets (using the end of the aisles for more impulse shopping), and more recently to improve health and wellbeing outcomes (changing where you can and can't smoke, workplaces changing the food within vending machines). In each of these examples, the individual is not restricted from participating in the activity; rather, doing so is more difficult.

Within our pop ups, we try to have an easier question or more introductory activity because once we have removed the initial barrier to participating, the likelihood that the participant will continue increases. An example of this might be an activity that requires someone to pop a sticker on a chart (dotmocracy) or a ball within a tube to vote.

In our opening address to people, as we say hello and introduce what we are doing, we try to hand them a ball or sticker and nudge them to participate. We also consider this through survey design. To reduce dropout rates within a survey, we often write in the demographic questions at the back and start with a few closed checkbox-style questions so participants experience momentum.

I appreciate this chapter might be met with some healthy scepticism. I would suggest starting small; start by first observing behaviour, body language and language. See if you can start to see, hear or feel patterns of behaviour.

What happens if they call you out on being Yoda?

We can all become a bit evangelistic when we learn something new (particularly when it works). For me, it comes back to the intent. If someone does get suss on your use of mirroring or feels the experience is manufactured, apologise and tell them why you are trying what you are doing – that is, to connect better with someone and to build trust and support them to participate. Let them know your intentions are pure, and ask them what support they need to participate.

What happens if you put them in the wrong box (learning system, core need)?

There will be signs! When used correctly, the conversation should feel easier and flow better. If you've assessed them incorrectly, the other person will start to feel frustrated and might become more tempered. I have done it plenty – thought someone was there for connection, only to offend them because it was really significance. They thought I was fluffing or wasting time. Change your tact quickly, match their tone and act with the same level of urgency they are displaying.

I dunno, it feels wrong and like I am invading their privacy.

Every day we are exposed to traditional 'directed' or 'enforced' interventions that have a basis in Nudge Theory or human behaviour. Think bins in a public space – a signal to put our rubbish in the bin.

Having a conscious understanding of the outcome we want to achieve allows us to use these behavioural theories to support participation, which will produce better outcomes for individuals and society.

The next chapter presents how to best design your pop up spatially. You can consider what you have learnt in this chapter to cater for the different learning needs and keep participants motivated to participate fully in your process.

Chapter 9

Rooms within rooms

When designing pop ups, I like to visualise them in 3D. I think about all the people that might visit, their different informational needs and the experiences they would prefer. In this chapter, I talk you through how we create different opportunities for people to have a uniquely different experience within the same pop up.

You and your friends are wandering down the main street, looking for a place to eat. You look in the window of a few places – one's super quiet, wait staff are folding napkins; one's super busy and a band is playing with bar seats at the window; the last one is half full with a corner booth available. Each restaurant will be attractive to someone while at the same time repel someone else. It is these individual tastes and preferences that we are trying to cater towards. It will depend on the reason for your visit. A catch-up with friends after some time apart? Perhaps the quiet restaurant offers a place to talk. A catch-up with work colleagues? The band might offer a nice diversion from work conversation. And you can think of whom you might take to the restaurant with the booth!

Just as there are different needs when sharing a meal with friends, so too are the different experiences sought out by our engagement participants. Some may seek answers to complex questions, others may seek to keep their contribution or involvement private, and still, some might not yet have an opinion and may wish to listen to or read the ideas of others before forming their own opinion.

The topic being discussed might require a different set-up – a project with more background information requires more inspired ways to display information to encourage readership; a project with less community interest might require something more novel or playful to attract attention; a project with significant community interest might require a larger space, fewer props and more experienced facilitators to lead multiple conversations.

Here are some benefits to tailoring your pop up design to suit the topic, audience or location you are in:

- **A range of participants is encouraged:** Creating an inviting set-up tailored to attract everyone – from your youngest stakeholders to your most invested community members – ensures that diverse perspectives are heard.
- **Ensured safety and accessibility:** Designing a set-up that suits the location, without creating obstacles or crowding, allows participants to engage comfortably and safely.
- **Right level of engagement:** Adding playful or interactive elements can spark interest where community engagement is low, while a more focused set-up for high-stakes or sensitive topics conveys respect and seriousness.

- **Varied engagement styles are supported:** Providing spaces for conversation, deep reflection and reading allows each participant to engage in the way that suits them best.
- **Ensured privacy for sensitive topics:** Offering confidential participation options – especially for topics like youth perspectives on vaping – makes it safe for everyone to share openly, even when sensitive information is involved.
- **Inclusive access is promoted:** Making your project accessible with clear visuals and straightforward language reduces barriers, encouraging participation from a broad range of people and building their confidence to engage.

Like in our example before, you're wandering down the main street, you see your Council's or water authorities branding on a banner; a small coffee van with people's hands wrapped around warm coffee mugs; people reading something on a large stand; others sitting at the front, having a conversation with someone official looking (not me); and someone warm and friendly at the front, talking to people about what is going on (me). Are you interested or do you hurry past, pretending to be on your phone?

Then, clear the screen. Now conjure in your mind a trestle table with some brochures, two people sitting behind it. Do you feel compelled to visit?

It is this decision we are trying to help people make. We want people to stop and talk to us, if not to participate in the project on the day. We want them to take away a card or scan the QR code on some signage so they participate at home. Considering that the set-up (Chapter 5) becomes even more critical in locations where people are in a more sceptical or rushed state (shopping centres, main streets), they are prepared to be approached by fundraisers, political campaigners and others stationed in the flow or walkway of people.

In this chapter you will learn to:
- create a clear entry point and exit point to assist people for self-service – an immediate hook to grab attention and hold interest and a lasting instruction to increase the reach of your pop up
- create zones within your pop up to cater to different participants' needs and levels of participation
- design the pop up for the location and other activities nearby, and make changes once onsite
- add in elements to either turn away or attract people to your pop up and when you might use these
- build up your pop up resource kit so you can continue to add materials and props to your set-up.

Create a clear entry point and exit point

Most projects need to give participants some information – how the project came about, what needs their attention or feedback and some sense of what happens next. Giving consideration to the sequence you want people to read this information can help define the layout. Having a clear flow of information – what is needed at the start, middle and end – can also help participants to move through the pop up when you get busy and allow them to self-service.

Start with a hook. I like a large sign that has the key project question or headline, which also helps describe what you are doing there.

You can have a short description to explain more and, if they don't have time to stop, a QR code linking them back to the project site or something to take away.

'We're replacing the playground at Made Up Reserve. Share your ideas for a more playful park!'

Next in your pop up journey will be some general project information – Why are you doing this? Is it part of a playground renewal program? Next comes the questions and additional information. Finally, it might be some information that describes what happens next – perhaps a 'Thanks for having your say.' or 'Let's keep the conversation going!' or 'Share this with your friends and family'. If you are outdoors and at the location for some time, you could use a footpath decal (though they often can't be reused).

Create zones and consider the spillover from activities

Like in my introductory story, people come to pop ups for different reasons. For some, it's the curiosity of seeing what is attracting others to your space. For others, it could be that they recognised your organisation's branding or signage and sought you out to discuss the project or something completely unrelated. Whatever the reason, you need to provide a space that can cater to these varied conversations.

Following are some spaces you might like to consider and the activities that could take place in these areas:

> **Reading nook:** Usually a quieter area where people can individually read or review project information and ask someone for advice if needed. Best if this is away from areas that are noisy.

Conversation zone: You might have a small table and chair, or it might be a standing room only. It's usually somewhere in the middle or end of the pop up journey, and people have already read the project information or participated and want to have a conversation about the project. This could be located close to the flow of foot traffic, unless it's a confidential conversation or likely to get heated. Being positioned at the front can help attract the people watchers who want to find out what it is all about.

Private participation: Some projects require people to bare their heart and soul – think of a young person describing the peer pressure they feel around smoking or vaping. You might want their participation to be away from prying eyes or family members, so you could create a secluded booth (think voting) or the caravan if you are using us!

Play zone: This could be a part of your hook to get people in; something closer to the front of your display in the flow of traffic that stops and invites interest. We often set up a quick question, and people respond by putting coloured balls in tubes.

Keep them occupied: Perhaps children and young people aren't the focus of your consultation, yet their parents, carers or grandparents are. You could set up a space in the middle that offers drawing, face painting or planting seedlings – activities that children can be occupied with and seen by their carers – allowing the caregiver to participate.

Be Cinderella in your pop up story

Design the pop up to suit the location and the other activities nearby. It can be easier to get the attention of passers-by when you are in a typical location (main street, in a park or reserve); your presence simply stands out and invites attention because you are not usually there.

When you set up in a farmers market or at an event or exhibition, you have to work harder to get attention, as it is already a visual feast for people. You are competing with some incredible visual merchandising, so you need to look the part if you don't want to be bypassed. This is when you might need to engage the support of a handy person to construct something eye-catching. Probably the best compliment I received was when we were consulting at a fair and were asked if there was a fee to participate in our activity. We were consulting on the redevelopment of an aquatic centre and created a structure where people stood underneath, pulled a cord, and a bucket of small bean bags flowed onto their heads. The squeals of happiness brought joy and attracted interest, so much so that we had a queue!

Touches to turn away or attract people

To attract the elusive young person or middle-aged person, you need to first lay the trap (free things). Be careful to stand downwind so they do not smell your fear, avoid eye contact at all costs and approach with casual ease. (Sorry, I went on a David Attenborough tangent.)

Sometimes the extra elements we add to attract a participant can repel a different group. It sounds awful, but out in my natural habitat, as someone without children, I will avoid places where there are children. I've had similar feedback from friends with children – when they are not with their family, they will also avoid places with children. If I see a set-up where there is face painting or a kids' drawing activity, I will not even look twice. My very efficient brain deems that experience as not for me. I won't even read the sign!

However, if I see a sign that says free coffee/plants/fruit, I'll be sceptical about the catch, but I love free stuff, so I will happily wander into the trap. Likewise, young people and people who look like them are lured in by my lollies and free food (from the further research in Chapter 8; explore the Law of Likeability).

So, consider the elements you add and whether they are likely to repel another user group. If they are, consider burying the gesture deeper within your set-up so they are not as obvious to other participants. There are some ideas in Chapter 11.

Create your base kit

At the end of this chapter I provide a couple of resources that can be used and recycled for any pop up. For me, the base kit is a frame sign that allows you to update and change the project inserts, teardrop banners or something that provides visual recognition from a distance and some easels and frames. All can be reused and repurposed and fit within the boot of a hatchback.

The temptation can be to leave the set-up conversation to the last minute; by then, the project team usually has run out of steam. They've been planning the project for some time, taking it to executive briefing and have discussed the purpose and intent at length, so they just want to get out there.

I would not blame you if, as you read through this chapter, you thought, *Do I really need to do all this?!*

It depends on your desired project outcomes. Even if your project is likely to attract significant interest, either because it's something everyone wants to see happen or are annoyed by it, you still need to think through the set-up.

Using the busy restaurant analogy from before, some people will walk straight past if they feel intimidated or are unable to see or find out what the project is about. When there is a project with significant interest, think through the flow of people – how can you keep people moving through the space or create a space within your floor plan where you can talk to people and leave the main project displays and information free for the less-informed. Avoid setting up on a narrow footpath if you know your project has high community appeal.

'But it's a small space!' Having a small space is not an excuse for not putting effort into the set-up. Often, shopping centre managers will only provide a small kiosk-sized space to project teams and will often require a render of how you intend to set up the space. At a minimum, you need to ensure good instant recognition – remember from Chapter 5, shopping centres are where people are most guarded, as they are used to fending off fundraisers (no offence to fundraisers' hearts). Lightweight banners, a frame signage and an easel or corflute cube structure should do the trick. All can be assembled in less than 30 minutes and carried in by hand or a shopping trolley! Avoid the temptation to bring a trestle table and chairs. Unless you have a face painter, don't sit behind a table.

'We can't expect staff to lug all this around.' We get it; not everyone can tow April the caravan with ease. You need a set-up that is easy to carry and can fit in the boot of a regular car. The shopping centre equipment can fit easily within a hatchback boot. I have provided some links to prop set-up to help with your research.

Chapter 10

Unpack on the day

You can do all the planning in the world, but if the delivery team doesn't implement what you have prepared and don't have the authority to make necessary tweaks, then you won't get the intended impact. In order for this to happen, we need to adequately hand over key information, check in during and debrief afterwards.

Given the often odd hours when pop ups are scheduled, it's likely that the team with all the project knowledge is not the team delivering the pop up. This is almost always the case in our line of work. There is often a project lead who might attend the first one to make sure it's running as planned. They then hand over the project to our Conversation Facilitators.

Getting this part of your final preparation right means:
- you are creating a safe space for your staff and members of the public

- staff working at the pop ups feel prepared and know what they are doing
- you have all the bits and pieces you need to do all of your planning justice
- you've built in enough time to set up, do site briefing and do final checks
- you are taking learnings from this experience into future pop ups
- you don't need to attend every pop up you plan.

You're setting up your future self nicely. Think about when you next put the call out to resource a pop up – people that worked last time will remember how easy it was, they knew where to park, wore the right footwear, arrived with plenty of time to unpack and gave you feedback (which you've added to your process for next time).

In this chapter you will learn to:
- create and use staff briefing materials so they arrive prepared and comfortable
- create and conduct a safety inspection to create a safe space for conversation
- create and use a staff debriefing process to embed your learnings from the day into future sessions
- give those working the pop up the freedom to make decisions on your behalf.

Transferring what you know into a briefing sheet

This is about setting up the delivery team with as much knowledge as you have about the project and location to do their job well.

It also means they have all the information to act with autonomy and make any necessary changes or tweaks to the delivery. We prepare a staff briefing sheet with location information for every pop up series. We don't typically do one for each location, but rather one for all the pop ups in the project.

Here is what we include in our briefing sheet:
- Project Overview: Information critical to the project – what it's about, any challenges or concerns with the project, what the conversation is about and key topics of conversation.
- Activity Plan: The way you intend to run the activities across your pop up and the combination of engagement activities you intend to include. Include copies of any surveys or key questions within your appendices.
- Staff Schedule: Details of who will be working at each of the pop ups, their contact details and timing of their shift.
- Location-specific Information: Address details, where to park and any site contacts or event organisers.
- What to Bring: If there are any specific materials that staff need to collect from a location or things you recommend they bring personally (food, water, etc.).
- What to Wear: Any uniform or protective requirements (closed-toe shoes, hat).

Creating a safe environment for staff and community

I'm not sure I need to provide a reason why you need to create a physically safe space for your conversation facilitators and members of the public. Working mostly outdoors, in sometimes crowded spaces, or spaces with traffic and multiple other uses increase the risk and complexity of working.

We've prepared a checklist tailored to the props and the set-up options we have within our pop up range, so while you can copy the format, you need to ensure that the elements within your checklist are specific to the set-up options you are proposing. A little of the risk assessment starts during your planning phase and site selection, and the majority happens during the pop up. Anything can change – a gust of wind, a dog running through your set-up or having more people than anticipated come into your set-up.

Here are some things to consider when designing your own safety checklist:

During set up:
- Unpack equipment using a safe handling technique, two people and a correct lifting technique.
- Set up any specific equipment in accordance with set-up requirements and ensure on flat, even ground.
- Ensure anything on the ground is not causing a trip hazard for you as you are setting up the equipment.

Before you open to the public:
- Check that the area around the pop up is clear and easily accessible for staff and the public to move around.
- Check that there are no hazards on the floor. If there are items on the floor, ensure they are identifiable and/or secured.
- Check that all items are secured and weighted down (signage, marquee).
- Are all personal belongings stored safely and out of public view?
- Does everyone onsite have the required checks (Working with Children Check, onsite inductions)?

Capturing and embedding the learnings from the day

It's the end of the day. It's been a long, but productive day with lots of good conversations. You've surveyed the area and double-checked to make sure everything has been brought in and packed away. The rumbling in your stomach draws your attention towards what's for dinner. Wouldn't it be tempting to call it a day and go home? Not so fast! The day is not complete without a debrief.

Do you all know how the day went? Well, maybe, but maybe not. Before you dismiss the importance of debriefing, consider the following advantages:

- **Time to reflect:** We are so busy doing and ready to move on to the next thing, that having dedicated time to reflect helps us and the people around us to consolidate experiences and consider perspectives from the participants' point of view.
- **We all hear and interpret information differently:** Just because we were all there doesn't mean we heard or interpreted information the same. The benefit of hearing different perspectives means you get a complete picture of how the day went.
- **Gain immediate feedback:** Debriefing with staff at the end of the day means the memories are not yet distorted or deleted, which is what our brain does. Also, it allows you time to make tweaks, if needed, when you are back in the office.
- **Remind the project team of their expertise:** Debriefing can also help consolidate knowledge. Hearing from others and sharing what they did in a situation can help people prepare for the next pop up or engagement session.

- **Value your staff:** Have you ever wondered what interesting conversations your staff have had that you're unaware of? Did they completely understand their role? Did they engage as well as they could have? The end-of-the-day debrief is a perfect time to have this conversation.

We've included a downloadable debrief document for you to adapt and use. Things to cover on your debrief are:

- Weather conditions: This can change the number of participants you might speak to and the outcomes of the day.
- Site conditions: Was the location quiet or busy? Was it loud, too narrow to set up or spacious and perfect for a pop up?
- Participant counts and details: Number of participants, age range, gender and any other defining characteristics.
- What worked well/didn't work well: What is your evidence for this (how do you know?)?
- Any improvement suggestions for future engagement activities.
- Engagement level: Were the participants willing to engage in the activity and have conversations about the project?
- Feedback collected on target: Were participant responses in line with what you needed from the day?
- Follow-up required: Are there any customer requests, general public questions or broken equipment that needs attending?

Is briefing staff really important?
You've got this far, and taking this final step might feel like a lot of extra work for little or no immediate returns. Or you might be worried that you are overcomplicating the experience for the

people who are working your pop up – getting them to read extra materials or coming along to a project handover might seem like overkill. You can offer up various ways to support them, and leave it to staff working the event to come. We always build in an additional 30 minutes of briefing/reading time and make it compulsory if the topic is more complex.

At a minimum, prepare and distribute the staff briefing pack. To encourage them to read more of it, write the email in a way that encourages them to open the attachment. What do most of us stress about? What to wear, where to park, what to bring. Writing 'Attached is information about the project, where to park, what to wear and what to bring with you on the day.' should increase readership.

You can make yourself available by phone or email in the lead-up to the event. If you are available on the day but can't physically be there, you might want to offer a backup call if needed. If you are unavailable, then provide a backup point of contact.

What happens if they need to change the pop up on the day?
Best to give one of the delivery team the authority to make changes or cancel the pop up and what to do if a change is needed. Circumstances when a change may be required:
- Weather (extreme heat or wet weather): Having a backup location is not always an option, particularly if your project is location-specific or you are going to provide walking tours as part of your engagement activity. Sure, there might be a rotunda onsite, but you are unlikely to have people venture outside during a storm or 40-degree day. Similarly, moving it without adequate notification might result in poor attendance.

- Something else happening onsite: There have been times when we have turned up to a pop up, and there are works going on onsite or access has been changed, making it difficult for people to access.
- Safety risks onsite: When working in public locations, we've had instances where there have been individuals under the influence of drugs or alcohol or have people unhappy with the project or process and trying to stop others from providing feedback.

In any of these situations, your onsite project lead may need to change the location of your pop up or reschedule it. This obviously has the potential to cause frustration in the community, and every attempt to minimise this needs to be made. Here are ways to do this on the day or the day before:

- Include any backup plans in the promotional posts for your project: 'In the event of bad weather, this event will be postponed or moved to [location].'
- Issue an update on your corporate channels if postponed or moved as soon as you know.
- Notify any nearby businesses of the change, as someone might ask them directly.
- If relocating, have someone stay close to the previous location (if safe to do so) and redirect people.

We have provided you with many of the resources we talked about in this chapter. They are ready for you to download, tweak and pop your logo on it. Visit www.conversationco.com.au/slpop to download:

- Staff briefing pack
- Debrief tool
- OHS checklist for you to think through the risks you have onsite

The next chapter discusses ways to avoid rejection and make sure you're not just talking to your colleagues about what to cook for dinner – as lovely as they are!

Chapter 11

We're not selling anything

Well, we kind of are selling them something – the hopes and promise of a better life or fairer and just world. But you can't say all that in 30 seconds! That's about all the time you have to grab and hold the interest of someone passing you.

Attention is a finite resource. While there are no conclusive studies on the number of ads the average person is exposed to daily, some quote it conservatively at 100, most in the thousands and, for more highly connected individuals, even as high as 4,000. Even at 100, this is already more competition than our projects can handle, so we need to use our smarts to compete for people's attention. You better have your elevator pitch ready for your projects as soon as you lock eyes with your potential participant.

I wouldn't be rich, but I would be able to treat myself to a nice meal for all the times I've been told 'I'm not interested', or worse, that we're 'not interested'. So, you think it's cool to be a civic blocker?

I feel like retaliating with 'Not interested in contributing to the betterment of society?' or 'Not interested in improving the lives of your children?'. I realise that makes me sound even more like a fundraiser, spruiker or salesperson, and I might as well be wearing a koala suit, as they are not coming back!

The rejection rate depends on the location of your pop up (read Chapter 5: 'Selecting the right location'). On average, we get one Not Interested for every three Sures. Shopping centres have the highest rejection, being on a main street can vary, and the illusive farmers market or civic event (think sustainability festival, children's event) is by far the nicest place. It really depends on the normal saturation of fundraisers or salespeople. One location was so bad, we were there for a week. We created a sign that said 'We're not selling anything'. It didn't work; I'm sure because that's what someone selling something would say.

Along with the advice within this book – site section and creating rooms within rooms – we've developed a few tricks and tips to keep that rejection rate lower so you can give yourself the best chance of speaking to as many people on the day as possible.

Reducing rejection and having a few strategies to reduce the rejection rate are not only good for you, it's a good thing for the general public. Planning to and reducing rejection will:
- help keep your self-esteem intact (or at least a little longer)
- make it easier to recruit more people to staff a pop up
- help more people participate in something they care about
- reach your wider engagement program aims through contact with your organisation – be that improved relationships, better awareness of your organisation or what you are doing.

- Better return on investment, making sure the time and resources invested in your pop up result in people talking to you.

In this chapter, you will learn ways to improve your chances of success:
- Generating interest before, during and after to leverage the FOMO effect.
- Leveraging your neighbours' relationships.
- Providing something they want for free.
- Being clear and identifiable.
- Having a solid elevator pitch for your project.

It will help if you think about this chapter through the lens of your sceptical general public self, not your civically minded farm market self. You're running late, you're multitasking, you haven't showered or brushed your teeth – whatever your public self is doing at, say, Saturday at 11 am. You hate being approached, not because you don't care about world issues; it could be something personal (you want to avoid being seen in your stained track pants, you're not wearing a bra), or it could be situational (you're out with family, on a new date).

Your reptilian brain is constantly scanning for risks and it spots not a dinosaur but one of those modern day risks – someone in matching uniforms on the street, blocking your path, very bubbly for this time of day and working hard to stop people. You can't get out of their direct line of approach – you're not a fast runner, you're a people pleaser – so if they do engage you, you'll be forced to say hi and nod while they talk to you for the 30 seconds it takes to cross their path. You remember your phone. You pull it out and have a fake yet animated conversation with yourself so it appears real.

Okay, you in that self? Great. Continue reading!

Generate interest before, during and after

This is why we need friends in high places or with connections to your organisation's corporate communication channels. You need to promote the heck out of what you are doing. The more times someone sees what you are doing, the more they are likely to remember it. So, get it in the local newspaper, online, through targeted social media ads, and if your project does not warrant that kind of attention or you've got zero dollars to do marketing, then print out some flyers and pop them up on the site you will be at. Be sure to tell any nearby businesses, at minimum. They will remember that someone from X organisation is coming down on Thursday afternoon. If you are setting up at a location, see if you can use the shopping centre, market or events advertising to promote what you are doing.

While onsite, make sure to take some photos and video recordings and send it to your friends with communication benefits. This will remind people that today is the day you are there and you are ready to engage (not sell). Take some photos of people you are talking to (don't forget to get their permission); this will help others see it as something they should be involved in.

After you have packed up, share any key learnings, images of people's notes and anything that causes people to think, oh we really should have gone down and had our say! Let's find out where the next one is.'

Leverage your neighbours' relationships

If you are at a location where you have neighbours (farmers market, shopping centre, shopping strip, event) go around to all the traders and have a chat about what you are doing. If the project intersects with their interests or they are impacted by it, then they can be your first subjects. Otherwise, leave some information with them so they can easily promote it to their regulars or clients. Give any perks of engaging – free coffee, free food, children's activities – so when they are asked 'What's going on out there?', even if all they remember is what organisation you are from, it will reduce your chances of rejection.

Make speaking to nearby businesses and/or traders a priority if you are near the vicinity of their entry way or business, as you do not want what you are doing at the front of their property to affect their trade or sales for the day.

Give them something they want for free

The sceptical self loves free stuff; caution goes out the window when something is free; partly because the **law of reciprocity** kicks in (Have fun googling it. See if you can read about how the Hare Krishnas use it, but only after this chapter; you are so close), mostly because we love free stuff. Before you order 1,000 branded mouse pads, the type of gimmick needs to align to the event, the target audience and the value assigned to the organisation or cause. Here are some examples and the situations they can be used in:

> **Give away free seedlings:** Nice environmental signal. Good for projects, brands or consumers who expect environmental

stewardship. You could combine this with an activity, planting it into a pot plant to create a vibe onsite.

> **Caution:** Get natives, as you do not want the complexity of gifting something from outside the area or something banned for your area. Consult with a local indigenous nursery.

Free face painting: Demonstrates the family-friendly nature of your organisation or project. Adds some vibrancy onsite as people wait in line and excited children dream up their designs. It also has lasting impact; other families will approach painted children, asking where they can find this elusive face painter.

> **Caution:** This will not attract (and it might deter) young adults, singles and couples with no children.

Free sunscreen: It's cheap and easy to provide, and on an unexpectedly hot spring day when people aren't yet prepared for the heat, it can be a family affair that triggers big-time reciprocity.

> **Caution:** Opt for a sensitive skincare brand. Make sure it is in date and that any children using it have the permission of a caregiver before use.

Free coffee: Either onsite (visible and attractive) or from a nearby trader or cafe. Free coffee or a hot beverage has high 'street appeal', particularly in Victoria. Like the face painting, people will tell others about it – 'Go and do the survey, and you'll get a free coffee!'

We often get people coming to us and saying, 'What do I need to do to get a free coffee?'. If you are supplying through a trader, you can always have someone located in the store or near the site and intercept people in the queue without looking like you are trying to pick them up.

> **Caution:** Don't supply free coffee from a van when there are traders nearby that your coffee would detract from.

If there are multiple cafes, try to provide a voucher that can be redeemed at any of them.

Free food: Attracts teenagers and children, which means the adults have to follow.

Caution: If your project is related to the environment, waste or health, avoid something high waste-producing or sugary (e.g., single-wrapped lollies). Opt for fresh fruit. Check any dietaries, and avoid items that can cause a severe allergic reaction (e.g., ingredients with nuts).

Be identifiable and look busy and interested

I should have mentioned that the 30 seconds starts when the potential participant first sees you – that's when the assessment of you and your stand starts. Again, think about your own actions in these scenarios:

Scenario 1: The kiosk, banners and displays are the colours of your health insurer. You get closer and can see the familiar branding. One person is sitting at a computer with a general public member. The person being spoken to or served looks like they are smiling, and it looks like they are free to leave at any time. There is another computer with an empty chair, and the other person is smiling at people passing by. There is a big sign that says, 'Don't keep paying for what you won't use. Update your policy today.' You've been meaning to update your policy as you no longer need some of the extras – ooh, they have free cupcakes because 'Everything in life with moderation' is their motto.

Scenario 2: You can't see anything identifiable, no colours or branding you recognise. There are two very energetic people moving into the flow of traffic to give people balloons on sticks. Others seem to raise their hand in a 'No, thank you' manner or are giving them a wide berth as they pass. You see a vague sign about energy policies and can't tell if it's an energy retailer or an organisation replacing LED lights (you've had a few calls at home). You don't think it's a government department either – balloons on plastic sticks don't convey the message.

Our brains are super smart and lightning-fast. At any moment, they draw on all of our previous experiences and the outcome of those experiences, then react in a manner that keeps us safe from a negative, awkward or time-wasting experience.

To enhance the chance of success, you need to convince the person's brain that it's okay, or at least engage their curiosity.

- Be identifiable and clear with who you are (use a frame or banners; make sure it is visible from both sides of the flow of foot traffic).
- Signage that clearly communicates why you are there – 'Have your say …', 'Tell us about …', 'Share your …' are all phrases that people associate with having their say.
- Keep busy. As soon as you have one person stop and talk to you, you're 'deemed safe'. If you have three or more people working your pop up, have one person approach people (or remain available) and the others looking busy – either reading the boards, talking to each other about the project or writing down some example ideas to prompt people. The fake action will entice others in and make it an easier sell. You can repeat this process during the quieter periods too.

Have a solid elevator pitch for your project

This is by far the hardest part – the part where you are opening yourself up to rejection, and it's the final three seconds of your 30-second interaction. You have the time it takes for a person to travel past your stall. I like to start as soon as they are in earshot, giving me five seconds.

You need to think about the person approaching and then connect what part of the project matters most to them to encourage them to stop and have their say.

This is where, if you have all of the other parts working for you (signage, fake participant plants, giveaways), you boost your chances. Don't waste your three seconds on filler words; include the question within your opening line – 'What matters most about …', 'What does xx need?'.

Usually, as a team we all try our own and then convene and talk about what is working best, particularly if our rates of success are lower.

Remember, don't take the rejection personally. I tell any new starters or project teams that it is a numbers game; the more interactions you have, the more rejection but also the more success you will have.

Are incentives a form of bribery?

After reading this chapter, you might be worried about using incentives. I have a research colleague that used to be so against using prize draws or providing any form of payment for surveys. Her theory was that it changes the motivation (why) for people providing feedback. Rather than coming from a place of interest, it comes from a place of getting the reward.

I like to think of it as honouring someone's time and contribution. There are many market research surveys (mystery shopper, product testing) that all provide a reward and, in my experience, it elevates people's participation.

We recently had a 10-minute activity and were giving away free coffee in exchange for completion. Those getting a free coffee completed all of it – either out of obligation (Law of Reciprocity) or treating it like a job – compared to others who completed one page of the activity. We also want people to participate in the project with different motivation levels; we want the highly interested and motivated, the disinterested and mildly interested, as they will each have different perspectives on our projects.

Should I just avoid shopping centres?

You might have picked up that shopping centres are tough environments for pop ups and think, *I don't think I will run a pop up at a shopping centre again*. Despite their challenges, they are well attended and enjoyed by the people we need to speak to. We need to go to where the people are and then do our best to invite interest and support their participation in our projects. They also provide an easy place to reach those commonly harder to reach like:

- young people hanging around a food court after school (imagine if you had free frozen yoghurt vouchers)

- pensioners and low-income earners visiting the shopping centre on a Thursday (aligned to the fortnightly payment calendar)
- families during school holidays (imagine if you provide a face painter)
- people, worried about the cost of living, escaping the heat on a 40-degree day.

With shopping centres, you need to think about your activity in a different way, as you are competing for interest (lots of attractive shops to look at), shoppers are on high scam alert, and there are different reasons for visiting – some are there for a quick meal purchase, others are filling in time.

What if I advertise?

Project teams often have concerns about promoting the project. The two biggest concerns are needing to change plans – due to weather or sickness in the project team – and if the pop up will be swamped by highly interested and engaged people. Promoting your project and your engagement activities is always the right approach. People participating is the ultimate goal, and we want to hear from a range of voices.

If there is no wet weather option and what you are doing is weather-dependent, then state that in your advertisement. In the event you do need to cancel, use your communication channels to provide an update. If you have to cancel because of staff illness, again provide an update on your communication channels. If someone can get down onsite and put up a 'Notice of change: Cancelled due to staff illness. Please contact …', then this will go a long way, as you don't want people walking the entire shopping centre, park or market and trying to find your stall only to not find you. You may get calls from unhappy people the next day, take the calls, apologise, explain the circumstances and offer an alternative method, either a one-to-one phone call with the project team or the next engagement opportunity.

Yes, highly interested and motivated people might attend your pop up project; it might be the most convenient option for them. Make sure you have more hands on deck so you can manage more detailed conversations while still inviting interest from members of the public. When planning your project, make sure there are multiple ways to participate in a project and advertise all of the engagement activities. Often, there is one workshop and more pop ups, so if they've missed the workshop date, then the pop up becomes the only remaining activity where they can speak to someone in person.

Chapter 12

Create your own proven formula

We are all on this learning journey together, and as our understanding and experience changes, so does our practice. I feel blessed to work with the people that I do, their level of self-awareness and reflection, and their commitment to improving our practice and the work we deliver.

My hope for you is that you create or strengthen the way community engagement is delivered in your organisation and, if you are starting from scratch, create your process for delivering pop ups.

Within one hour, you will have forgotten an average of 50% of the information you've learnt. Within 24 hours, 70% of new information will be gone, and 90% within a week. These stats drop significantly if you take action on what you have learnt, so completing the activities after each chapter will help to reduce this. You can, of course, go back to any chapter at any time for a refresh or to specific chapters where you think your process needs a little extra tightening. Making changes to your internal processes and procedures as you go will retain the new knowledge you've gained reading the Secret Life of Pop Ups.

Benefits of creating, adding to and revisiting your own proven process area:

- You will no longer be the sole holder of this knowledge and called upon to deliver everyone else's pop ups. Go crazy and book a massage for a Saturday in the future.
- Customers, community and stakeholders will know what to expect when they see your organisation out in the community.
- Everyone in the organisation will use and strengthen one process, not individual processes held within their own team or unit.
- Management loves a process. If you can show them why you need something like a physical prop, storage for physical materials or budget for communication, or why you need to get external support or a hire dedicated to community engagement delivery, then you will have a better chance in winning your case.

The risk is that you, the reader, become the sole holder of this knowledge – the unicorn that every time **you** deliver pop ups, they turn out 'so well' for 'some reason'! I would rather you get your accolades from creating a process that is easy for others to follow and implement than being the one who worked the most Saturdays in the year.

In this chapter you will learn to:
- engage sensitively with possible process owners to create or iterate an existing process for delivering pop ups
- prioritise what to work on first, based on the way community engagement is delivered in your organisation
- draw on the experiences of others, encourage experimenting and encourage process users to alter or add to the process
- build organisation support and capacity to deliver the process and provide training in gaps
- make friends within your organisation to strengthen your cause.

You are not their saviour

Love the enthusiasm, but before you re-enter your organisation (book in hand, of course), holding all the answers, do some enquiring as to what processes, resources or tools exist. Unless, you're the go-to person or a part of the go-to team and know there isn't already a process in place. This is the disclaimer I wish I had sometimes for life in general!

How is community engagement delivered in your organisation? Is it through a decentralised system, where every team or unit is responsible for planning and delivering their own engagement? Or is it through a centralised function or team, where you need to seek permission, schedule in your engagement, then get internal support for the planning and delivery of community engagement projects? This will help you know who and how many people to involve in the first place. How you manage this part really depends on the situation within your organisation.

Here are some potential next steps based on the current scenario.

You own the process, or the process owns you (Hello, road to getting your Saturdays back!)

Pull together others that also own, interact with (communications) or regularly deliver pop ups. Document what happens step by step in the lead-up to delivering a pop up, during the running and after pop ups are delivered. You can do this online or you can lock yourself in a room together with snacks. Pull out four-coloured or differently shaped Post-it notes, and write down key steps.

A good tool for this is a Customer Journey Process – type it into any search engine, and there will be a heap of tools and readings on this. If online, Miro or Atlassian offer great templates.

Think about the process from the perspective of your 'customers'. In this process, it would be your internal customers whom you either support to deliver consultation themselves or deliver for them, depending on your delivery set-up. The other customer type is the people who provide their wisdom at the pop ups.

Have one coloured Post-it note for each customer type; your needs and ideas will come in next! For each customer type, keep asking the group:
- What happens before that? – to get to the start of the process
- What triggers that to happen? – to see what other processes intersect this
- What happens next? – to get to the end of the process.

Document each of these responses on Post-it notes so you can move them around if there is a step that comes before or after. You then need to think about **pain points** – for you or your customer – and their possible solutions.

Some examples of pain points for your internal customers who deliver pop ups:
- Not knowing the lead-up time required to ensure any pre-work for pop ups – graphic design, booking in resources or getting support with communications.
- Not knowing if pop ups are a good fit for their topic or project and when to use them.

Some examples of pain points for your external customers who attend pop ups:
- Not knowing when there is a pop up near them.
- Pop ups not being on times or in locations they can attend.

Are there any other process users (customers) or owners you need to speak to? Have you spoken to a range of customers, including someone new to the organisation or someone who has been there for some time? What about maintenance who are required to store or help set up your props?

During this time, you'd want to bring everything together that you or people in your organisation are already doing and look at what is missing or could add value. Remember to use any data collected from your community, clients or customers to understand how they prefer to engage with your organisation and anything that relates to delivering in-person engagement.

Once you are happy you've documented what happens currently, it doesn't need to stay like this. You can move around the steps or create others (don't overcomplicate it, though) to make it run smoother and perhaps remove some of the pain points. So, again with your brains, list out and identify the process and some of the likely triggers that might prompt someone to use it. When I was an internal resource, we had ready-made boxes of great pens and Post-it notes for people to take out in the field. We were in a decentralised system but still needed some oversight; sometimes it would be the first time we would find out about a project happening in the field. Until the process is up and running and commonplace, you will have people entering your process at different times.

Okay, grab a cuppa and then head down to prioritising.

If you don't own the process, you need to find out who does
You need to find out if there is a team or person responsible for delivering community engagement. Usually, the people who care the most about this sit within communications or customer service, as they most likely need to deal with the fallout and answer customer enquiries or complaints if something goes wrong. Otherwise, you could start by doing a search of your intranet or your corporate website, see if there are any community engagement tools, a community policy or framework, and then track down the owner. Then, sensitively ask how one would go about getting some support to deliver pop ups for their own projects. Is there any process they would follow or support?

If there is a process, and you haven't yet used it, probably start by using it or seeing if anyone in your team has used it. You then might compare the process with some of the ideas within this book and approach the owner with an offer of assistance or brainstorming. Maybe take them out for coffee before you ask if they wanna be your new BFF and lock themselves in a room with you – with snacks and some Post-it notes, of course.

'Can we grab coffee one day? I have read a book, and I want to work with you to create a process for delivering pop ups and intercepts that makes it easier for staff to follow and gives the community a good experience.'

There is no process or person/people responsible
You've done some digging, and community engagement does not exist in your organisation. It could be that your organisation doesn't have a need for it or doesn't know it is needed. If you do feel there is a need, even if you are a senior leader in your organisation, you have to build the case for why time and resources should be put towards strengthening your community engagement approach.

My advice would be to see if people are informally delivering community engagement. They might be on the promotional side of engagement, wherein the community provides them with information only or advises them of a decision. There could be some who are speaking with people directly affected or interested by a decision. If there is enough interest, then create a working group from people across the organisation and go about creating the process; you can use the Customer Journey Process identified in the section above. You then need to find or create opportunities to test the process to see if the steps you have put in place are in logical order and the support that is required.

Prioritise what to work on first

For this section, I am going to assume you have mapped out your process. Put a coloured dot on the Post-it note to help you easily identify what currently exists, needs creating or can be tweaked to fit the new process. The level of experience your organisation has with delivering community engagement will influence the number of tasks you have to get your process up and running. You then need to look at what needs to be created or tweaked and decide what to do first. To help you decide, you might want to consider what matters most. Here are some things to consider:

- Improving the safety of participants and staff.
- Making it easier for others to deliver their own engagement.
- Reducing the risk of negative media attention and complaints to your organisation.

Another way to approach this is by looking at the skills, interests and expertise of the team or group of people you brought together to help create the process. Remember to use the templates and any of the completed examples from within this book.

Make friends within your organisation
Engagement really does reach across many different departments. While you are working through your to-do lists and strengthening your process, remember to build relationships with the other people and teams your work intersects with.

Here are some friends you are going to need to make (if you haven't already):

- Maintenance or depot staff: Essential to assist with storage of large props, repairs and assistance with set up of marquees and displays.
- Internal communications staff: Help build relationships and promote and encourage the use of the new process you are creating.
- External communications staff: They will have their own process for promoting pop up activities to the community and their own lead times for delivering marketing activities.

Encourage experimenting and encourage process users to alter/add to the process

With your draft process complete, key tools, templates and activities drafted, you need to keep your process alive and update it as your knowledge and experiences grow. A couple of ways you can do this is by:

- building in reviews to check in on process users who have started to use the process – What is working? What feels clunky? What is missing?
- experimenting with alternatives before you formally launch your process to the wider organisation. Get an experienced few to test what works and what things work in different environments.

Build organisation support and capacity to deliver the process

Once you are happy with the process you've created and tested and are ready to embed it into the organisation, you need to get people excited and comfortable with using it. Here are some ideas:

- Launch an event with an overview of the process, how and where to get support, and tools available.
- Training across different levels, you could add yourself into the final 10 minutes of a team meeting, provide lunchtime learning sessions, or provide department training.
- Pull together a group of process champions and have representatives from each department; a drawcard could be that you provide other certified engagement training.

Remember to keep the process alive by sharing updates, learnings and good news stories across the organisation via an intranet or regular staff communications.

Afterword

Writing this book has been an exciting journey – a chance to pull together insights, stories and lessons that I hope will make a real impact in the field of community engagement. I set out to create something practical, a resource that goes beyond theory and gives professionals the tools to develop their own approach to delivering face-to-face engagement. Above all, I want readers to walk away with a newfound respect for in-person engagement and an understanding of how a well-structured process can transform community programs, deepening their reach and strengthening their purpose.

One of the most memorable aspects of this journey has been reflecting on the countless experiences I've had out in the field. In community engagement, you meet people in all their forms. I think of the farmer, vulnerable and open about the devastating impact of drought on their livelihood, or the child who shares a hopeful vision of their future. I've had the privilege of supporting project managers as they bring their ideas into the community and find joy when someone truly connects with their work. There's a sense of responsibility that comes with this role – almost like being a Santa Claus for adults, entrusted with people's most personal wishes and fears. My biggest challenge has been ensuring that these stories reach those who need to hear them. Every story, every interaction feels like a trust that must be honoured.

In writing this book, I've come to appreciate my own journey as a practitioner, recognising the expertise I've built over the years. I've also developed a deeper appreciation for my talented team at Conversation Co, past and present, who have helped shape and improve our practice. This book is, in many ways, a tribute to everyone who has contributed to Conversation Caravan and Conversation Co. Their dedication has amplified our impact, and I'm grateful for the opportunity to share a bit of that experience here.

Looking ahead, I see a future for community engagement and social research that elevates the pop up experience without losing its simplicity. While I hope pop ups gain more sophistication, I don't want them to become so complex that they're no longer approachable. Setting up a strong, visually appealing and relevant community presence takes time – planning, designing, creating props, printing materials and finding the right location. My hope is that this book will encourage professionals to invest the six to eight weeks of preparation that truly effective pop ups need, drawing inspiration from marketing, event planning and retail pop ups to engage the public in fresh and compelling ways.

If there's one takeaway I hope readers gain, it's the importance of creating and refining a process that works for them and sharing it with others. I want this to be a living resource, one that grows as people add their own insights, expand on it and adapt it to their unique contexts. Community engagement thrives on collaboration, and I hope this book inspires readers to build something that lasts.

Acknowledgements

The world is a better place thanks to those who have fought and continue to fight for change. Early in my career, I was awestruck by a chance meeting and talk from Janet Price, who shared her experiences with the Franklin Dam and her ongoing push for environmental reform. Her story taught me that community engagement is, in many ways, polite activism – a way for the public to influence and inform change beyond election cycles.

To everyone striving to improve the practice of community engagement – whether by advocating for better resources within an organisation, refining processes, or sharing skills and experiences – thank you. To the individuals I've worked with, or spoken to on the street, thank you for trusting me with your stories and investing your time to make your community, your life or the lives of future generations better. Without your voices, and the support of my peers and mentors, this book would not exist.

Having an idea and turning it into a book is as challenging as it is rewarding. I especially want to thank those who made this journey possible. My deepest gratitude to Drew Holman for his (mostly) unwavering support of my journey with Conversation Caravan, which gave me the insights and experiences to write this book. To Kate Berg for her beautiful cover design, and to Kate Wilby, Jenny Grogan, Ella West, Sachi Florance and Jacqui Goy for their invaluable contributions—whether through content, resources or brainstorming when I needed it most. Thank you to Harley Nguyen and Kristie Loke for their creativity in bringing this book to market, even as deadlines kept shifting. Finally, to the entire team at Conversation Co, past and present: your dedication, processes, and innovations have shaped many of the resources now available to readers.

About the Author

After more than a decade in community and stakeholder engagement, Cindy Plowman has experienced the realities of fieldwork – rain or shine – navigating the intricate dynamics between people and projects. As the Director of Conversation Co., Cindy brings a fresh, innovative approach to face-to-face engagement, from her earlier career in event management and marketing, using creative pop-ups and thoughtful design to bridge the gap between communities and decision-makers.

With expertise spanning social infrastructure planning, environmental planning and development, policy reform and health promotion, Cindy has collaborated with government agencies, not-for-profit organisations and private enterprises. Her unique perspective has redefined traditional engagement practices, transforming them into opportunities for genuine connection, learning, and lasting impact.

Cindy has witnessed the transformative power of in-person engagement – from the farmer candidly sharing his struggles with drought to the project manager who, with guidance, finds their voice and fosters meaningful connections with their community.

Free downloads to get you on the way

There are some great resources that have been developed by team Conversation Co/Caravan across the years, so head to www.conversationco.com.au/slpop to download these.

Notes